I Knit Paris

Rebecca —
Always knit
like a local ☺
Bon tricot!
Kathleen
& Alice

ONE
MORE
ROW
PRESS

New York • Washington

I Knit Paris

Editors: Kathleen Dames & Alice O'Reilly
Pattern Photographer: Clara Ferrand
Art Director & Graphic Designer: Kathleen Dames
Technical Editor: Laura Cameron
Illustrator: Laurel Johnson
Stylist/Photography Assistant: Lucile Francomme
Model: Alisson Corteggiani
Paris Photographers: Kathleen Dames & Alice O'Reilly

Designers: Christelle Bagea, Enrico Castronovo, Marion Crivelli, Marie Amélie Designs, Julie Dubreux, Chloé Fourtune-Ravard, Lucile Francomme, Sara Maternini, and Sylvie Polo

Yarn Support: La Bien Aimée, De Rerum Natura, La Fée Fil, Maison Corlène, Les Petits Points Parisiens, Polo & Co., Tôt Le Matin, (Vi)laines, and Yarn by Simone

Copyright © 2018 One More Row Press
Photographs copyright © 2018 Clara Ferrand
Illustrations copyright © 2018 Laurel Johnson
All rights reserved. Patterns are for personal use only and not for resale or sharing. No part of this publication may be reproduced or transmitted in any form or by any means, electronic, mechanical, photocopying, recording, or otherwise, without prior written permission from the publisher.

Printed in the United States, United Kingdom, and Australia by IngramSpark.

ISBN: 0-692-18896-5

Direct all inquiries to *hello@onemorerowpress.com*.

Follow One More Row Press
Facebook: *fb.me/onemorerowpress*
Instagram: *@onemorerowpress*
Pinterest: *onemorerowpress*
Sign up for our newsletter on our website: *onemorerowpress.com*

To download, redeem at *ravelry.com/redeem/one-more-row-press*

IKPOMRTSKMW687

A note about needles and gauge

The needle sizes and circular needle lengths specified in each pattern are those used by the designers to knit the items you see photographed on the following pages; they are not necessarily the sizes and lengths *you* will need to make yours. Use the needle size that allows you to achieve gauge.

We know it may not be your favorite thing, but we highly recommend a gauge swatch for all projects to avoid disappointment. For the garments, why not start a sleeve? If you achieve gauge, you already have part of a sleeve finished, and if you don't, it's not a huge amount of knitting. Don't forget to block your swatch before measuring your gauge.

If you prefer knitting small circumferences with the Magic Loop method, you will be most comfortable with needles that are 40 inches/100 cm or longer (Magic Loop can be done with 24-inch/60 cm needles, but longer is more comfortable) in the size that allows you to achieve gauge. DPNs, two circulars, or short circulars are all viable options, so choose what works for you. For garments, especially those worked in the round, choosing a needle length *slightly* shorter than your desired circumference will make for a comfortable knitting experience for the body.

A note about yarn

We love the yarn choices our designers made for each pattern but know that it may be more difficult to find said yarns wherever you are in the world. To help you make yarn substitutions, we include yarn weight and fiber content in each pattern, as well as approximate meterage. France uses the metric system, but we have included Imperial measurements, too. On each pattern you will find a small green box with contact information for the company whose yarn was used, in case you would like to engage in some international commerce.

Contents

Bonjour, tricoteur!*

*Tricoteur (n): Knitter. See also tricot, tricoté, tricoteuse.

"Paris is always a good idea," said Audrey Hepburn as **Sabrina**, and we couldn't agree more. To create the ultimate knitting-in-Paris-experience, we asked a few of our favorite French designers to create their version of Paris in knits and purls. Whether you think of the City of Light in terms of history, landmarks, fashion, or the movies, we've got something for you.

In addition to ten gorgeous patterns you will want to knit up *tout de suite*, we have a tour our favorite Paris yarn shops, from the 1° to the 18° Arrondissement, with a few non-yarn places we know you will enjoy, too.

We love giving a group of designers the same inspiration because they always come up with wildly different designs in lace, cables, and colorwork. Inside these pages you will find not one (from **Marie-Amélie Designs**), not two (from **Julie Dubreux, a.k.a. Julie Knits In Paris**), but three (from **Marion Crivelli**) Eiffel-Tower-inspired knits, yet each is very much its own design. While *La dame de fer* always lights up Paris, **Tricot et Stitch's Christelle Bagea** reminds us of the soaring beauty of Notre Dame, **Chloé Fourtune-Ravard** of **Tisserin Coquet** and **Julie Dubreux** give us two different perspectives on *les jardins* of this blooming city, and both **Sara Maternini** of **La Cave à Laine** and **Les Tricoteurs Volants** owner **Enrico Castronovo** turn the endless stairs of Montmartre into knitwear. To ensure you are dressed for Paris, we have sailor stripes from **Lucile Francomme** and a charming beret by **Sylvie Polo**.

We chose to work with a variety of French yarn companies for *I Knit Paris*, from hand dyers and shop owners **La Bien Aimée** and **Les Petits Points Parisiens** to **De Rerum Natura**, with their breed specific yarns, to our designer Sylvie, who hand dyes her yarn in Normandy under the sign **Polo & Co.** Thanks to our designers (and our time in Paris) we also got to know the beautiful yarns of **La Fée Fil, Maison Corlène, Tôt Le Matin, (Vi)laines**, and **Yarn by Simone**.

Whether you are armchair travelling/knitting or visiting the City of Light, we hope you enjoy *I Knit Paris*. As they say when you depart the Parisian yarn shops...

Bon Tricot!

Alice & Kathleen
Editors, One More Row Press

P.S. Be sure to share your knits with *#iknitparis* on Instagram and tag us *@onemorerowpress* with your *I Knit Paris* projects.

Knitting in Paris

Things to know before you go...

- Appreciation for the act of knitting in Paris is a little behind what we are used to in the States. Some café staff were unhappy to see knitters occupying their tables, considering it a private activity, although staring moodily or scribbling in a notebook would not be a problem. Attitudes are changing, though, and we were treated just like everybody else in almost all the cafés we visited. The café in question did not mention anything to us but did voice their opinion to our French companions, who were understandably upset. We say knit as you like but know that not everyone appreciates the wonders of knitting.
- All shops we visited accept major credit cards, though they are, of course, happy to take your Euros.
- Tax is included in prices, including yarn/ needles/notions. You may want to research VAT (Value Added Tax) rebates, though in our experience you would have to buy quite a lot of wool at a shop to qualify.
- Shops are often closed on Sundays and/ or Mondays (but not all of them), so be sure to check shop websites/social media/ Google Maps for opening hours and days. Summer is a lovely time to visit Paris, but many shops close for vacation for part of August.
- Classic commercial French yarn lines include Bergère de France, DMC, Fonty, Plassard, and Phildar, which has quite a few shops in Paris. Not too long ago commercial yarns were even sold at **Le Bon Marché** (imagine shopping for yarn at a department store). With our bias towards hand-dyeing, we focused on LYSes that stock indie dyers and more unusual yarns.

Vocabulary

les aiguilles = needles   la laine = wool
l'alpaga = alpaca   le lin = linen
le bouton = button   ouvrir = open
les ciseaux = scissors   le pull = pullover
le coton = cotton   le ruban = ribbon
une écharpe = scarf   la soie = silk
fermé = closed   tricoter = to knit

Au revoir = Goodbye (literally, until we meet again; do not use *adieu*, which is *very* final)
Avez-vous plus de cela? = Do you have more of this?
Bonjour = Hello (use this *everywhere* and with everyone—not saying hello is considered very rude)
Combien ça coûte? = How much is this?
De rien = You're welcome (literally, "it was nothing")
Excusez moi = Excuse me
Je ne parle pas Français = I don't speak French
Je regarde = I'm (just) looking
Je suis désolé = I'm very sorry
Merci (beaucoup) = Thank you (very much)
Pardon = Sorry
Parlez vous Anglais? = Do you speak English?
S'il vous plaît = Please

Knitting Groups

Tricoter à Paris
Group regularly meets for knitting with a glass of something. Check *facebook.com/ tricoterparis* or @tricoterparis on Instagram for details.

Les Petits Points Parisiens
Knit Night every Thursday in the shop. Details at *ravelry.com/groups/les-petits-points-parisiens*

L'OisiveThé
Wednesday evening Knitting Salon for 22 lucky people. Sign up at *ravelry.com/groups/ loisivethe-salon-de-the-et-tricot*

A note about shopping in Paris

In our experience most shopkeepers and staff speak some English, but it is polite to attempt some French. When you walk into a shop, say "Bonjour!" If that's all you can manage, switch to English and look around.

When shopping be patient. Parisians don't mind a queue for good service, so expect to stand in a line to wait for a clerk to assist you (particularly at longer-established shops, which tend to be set up with counters, as opposed to what you may be used to at an American yarn shop). Once it is your turn, they are all yours.

Clerks want to help you (it is their job and they take pride in what they do), and they do not want you messing up their stock, so do ask for help or let them know you are just looking.

We hear all the time from knitters shopping in Paris that this shop or that was rude, but we did not find that to be the case. Americans tend to expect to walk into any shop, anywhere, and make friends—it is just how we are in the world. What the French offer is expertise.* They are not there to be friends but to help you find what you need. That being said, we found most clerks and shop owners to be friendly and welcoming. Perhaps knitting is the new *lingua franca*?

Our advice: Always say, "Bonjour," manage your expectations, and you will have an excellent Parisian shopping experience.

*You will find this same pride in one's job and expertise everywhere in France, especially with waitstaff in restaurants (perhaps not at the corner café—your mileage may vary). If your waiter encourages you to have that apple crisp with cream, have it with the cream. If you cannot have the cream (for whatever reason), choose another dessert. Same goes for clerks in shops. They really do know what they are talking about, and they want you to thoroughly enjoy your meals and purchases.

Paris is organized into twenty arrondissements, swirling out and around from the western tip of Île de la Cité like a snail shell, beginning in the center with the 1° where you will find Les Jardin des Tuileries, Le Louvre, and Le Palais-Royal, then ending at Père Lachaise Cemetery in the 20°.

For our listings, we noted the arrondissement of each yarn shop, as well as the address, to help you find your way, and the shops are grouped according to how we visited them. For instance, we visited Les Petits Points Parisiens then walked (downhill) to Les Tricoteurs Volants (both on p. 43). You could also walk from LTV to Lil Weasel, which isn't far from Sajou and La Droguerie (pp. 7 & 8). La Bien Aimée even has a charming postcard showing you the way to L'OisiveThé (both on p. 49).

Add these shops to your favorite map app before you go, or visit Kathleen's map: goo.gl/maps/FpHA1V6q6M42 It includes all the shops in this book, plus a few more we plan to visit next time. Because with Paris, there is always a next time.

La Droguerie à Paris
9 & 11, rue du Jour, 1° Arr. • Tél: +33 1 45 08 93 27
Website: ladroguerie.com • Instagram: @la_droguerie

You can't miss the colorful storefront that houses the Parisian branch of La Droguerie (they have nine other shops in France, plus five in Japan). Walk inside and discover the craft "drugstore" of your dreams: buttons, beads, ribbon, jewelry findings, and so on. They have their own line of yarn and will wind off your desired amount of yarn from cones, plus they have their own range of knitting and sewing patterns. Set up like a 19th century apothecary, queue up at the counter you are interested in and wait for a clerk to help you. When it is your turn, your clerk will help you for as long as you need and with everything in the store. Your patience will be rewarded. La Droguerie gets very crowded, so if you can, visit first thing.

Au pied de cochon, open 24 hours a day, is on the corner, and E. Dehillerin (where Julia Child stocked her kitchen) is on the next block. You are also near the former Les Halles market (now an underground mall), with the Louvre to the west and the Pompidou to the east.

2° Arr: Lil Weasel

2° Arr: Sajou

Lil Weasel
1 & 4, passage du Grand Cerf, 2° Arr. • Tél : +33 1 73 71 70 48
Website: lilweasel.com • Instagram: @lilweasel

Situated in one of the charming *passages* you will find on the Right Bank (covered shopping arcades, most built in the first half of the 19th century), Lil Weasel is actually two shops across the way from one another, plus an *atelier* upstairs from the woolier side for knitting and sewing classes. The knitting shop opened in 2010, and Carine started dyeing yarn in 2016. In addition to the Lil Weasel line, you will find Fonty, La Fée Fil, (Vi)laines, and more, plus needles, buttons, and bags. The fabric shop, which opened in 2015, stocks fabric from Liberty of London, Cotton + Steel, and others, plus bias tape, plenty of notions, and cute enamel pins.

There are other charming shops in the passage (and we hear the Christmas decorations are not to be missed), so be sure to walk on from Lil Weasel, and don't forget to look up to the glass ceiling—the unusual third floor is all apartments. En route from here to Sajou we discovered **Sitron**, *a tasty little gluten-free patisserie, on Rue Marie Stuart.*

Sajou
47, rue du Caire, 2° Arr. • Tél: +33 1 42 33 42 66
Website: sajou.fr • Instagram: @maisonsajouofficiel

While not a Local Yarn Shop *per se*, you will not want to miss Sajou. Looking for the perfect pair of embroidery scissors, a bit of ribbon, or a portion of the Bayeux Tapestry to cross stitch? Make your way to their orange facade and prepare to want all the things. The shop's wooden drawers (reproductions of which are also for sale, along with miniature versions) are filled with charming treasures, largely with a focus on sewing, cross stitch, and embroidery, but they do stock some yarn and needles, too, along with a selection of knitting and sewing books. They also offer sewing, embroidery, and knitting classes.

Be sure to take a peek at the **Passage du Caire** *across the way. It is the oldest covered arcade in Paris, built in 1798 and decorated with three statues to the Egyptian goddess Hathor at the entrance.*

Though we weren't able to stop by, a number of Parisians mentioned **G. Detou**, *nearby, for baking supplies and memorable yet unconventional souvenirs.*

Marie-Amélie loves Paris

What has your knitwear design journey been like?

I started to create my own knitwear design two years ago (after one year of passionate knitting) because I wanted to create patterns which are fashionable with great attention given to the construction, a flattering fit, and details that make a garment feminine and modern. Before designing, and even knitting, I was an avid sewer for almost 10 years and this hobby gave me confidence to make handmade garments that reflect my style and are better than what I find in my favorite ready-to-wear shops.

With my knitwear designs, I want knitters to feel accomplished and to be proud of their gorgeous knitted garments.

Tell us a Paris story...

Until the second part of the 20th century, there was a covered fruit and vegetable market at the heart of Paris called **Les Halles**. Breton Farmers who sold garlic in this market wore large pullovers knitted by their wives. Those *Marchands d'ail* (garlic merchants) gave their name to *chandail*, which is a word for pullover in French. While *chandail* is not often used in France anymore, it remains the way to designate sweaters in Quebec.

Top Ten Movies

1. Le Fabuleux destin d'Amélie Poulain 2. Les Bronzés 3. Le Cercle des poètes disparus 4. Les 3 frères 5. Forrest Gump 6. Gran Torino 7. La Vie est belle 8. Edward aux mains d'argent 9. Tout sur ma mère 10. La Guerre est déclarée

Top Ten Songs

As I could not choose ten songs, here are my favorite 10 (+ 1) French songs about Paris

1. Jacques Dutronc—*Il est cinq heures Paris s'eveille* 2. Serge Gainsbourg—*Le poinçonneur des Lilas* 3. Matthieu Chedid and Vanessa Paradis—*La Seine* 4. Charles Aznavour—*La Bohème* 5. Thomas Dutronc—*J'Aime Plus Paris* 6. Louise Attaque—*Les Nuits Parisiennes* 7. Edith Piaf—*Sous Le Ciel De Paris* 8. Jacques Brel—*La Valse à Mille Temps* 9. Pigalle—*Dans La Salle Du Bar Tabac De La Rue Des Martyrs* 10. Alain Souchon—*Rive Gauche* 11. France Gall & Michel Berger—*Ça Balance Pas Mal À Paris*

Top Ten Books

1. Albert Cohen—*Belle du Seigneur* 2. Romain Gary—*La promesse de l'aube* 3. Joël Dicker—*La vérité sur l'affaire Quebert* 4. Alice Ferney—*La conversation amoureuse* 5. Muriel Barbery—*L'élégance du Hérisson* 6. Mary Ann Shaffer and Annie Barrows—*Le cercle littéraire des amateurs d'épluchures de patates* 7. Elena Favilli—*Histoires du soir pour filles rebelles: 100 Destins de femmes extraordinaires* 8. Christelle Dabos—*Le passe miroir* 9. Hélène Grémillon—*Le confident* 10. Delphine de Vigan—*Rien ne s'oppose à la nuit*

Top Ten TV Shows

1. The Bold Type 2. The Marvelous Mrs Maisel 3. Sense8 4. Anne with an e 5. Peaky Blinders 6. Call the Midwife 7. Downton Abbey 8. Alias Grace 9. Atypical 10. Outlander

Métro knitting: must-have or never ever?

I love to knit on public transportation. Since you can do very little on the Métro, I like to think I save time by knitting while riding. I try to quickly get a seat (if nobody is more in need than me, of course). I usually listen to an audio podcast when I knit in the Métro, but if someone wants to ask me about what I am knitting, I am more than happy to start a conversation. Unfortunately, it does not happen often.

Favorite station? Favorite Neighborhood?

Arts et Métiers in the 3°. **Le marais.**

Picker or thrower?
Project monogamy or cast on all the things?

Picker. Cast on all the things trying to become monogamous.

Favorite places to eat/drink/knit in Paris?

I love Parisian parks, so I grab a sandwich in a good *boulangerie* and sit on a bench to eat, knit, and watch life happening in front of me. One of my favorite parks to do so is **Palais-Royal** in the 1° or **La Place des Vosges**, straddling the border between the 3° and 4°. To have a drink, I love all the bars near the **Bastille** in the 11°.

La Dame de Fer Cardigan
by Marie-Amélie/Marie Amélie Designs

Constructed for the 1889 World's Fair in Paris, the Eiffel Tower is a wrought iron lattice structure rising 324 meters above the Seine. Each piece of the "Iron Lady" was constructed at a factory in the Parisian suburb, Levallois-Perret, and brought to the Champ de Mars site on horse-drawn carts, and only the decorative arches at the base of the tower were not essential to the structure. Every one of the 18,038 pieces of iron were precisely engineered to fit together perfectly (rivet holes for the 2.5 million rivets had to be drilled within 0.1 mm to ensure that the tallest-at-the-time man-made structure would be wind-resistant).

Though controversial when built and only expected to stand for 20 years, the Eiffel Tower is one of the world's most-recognized and most-visited structures. Guy de Maupassant supposedly ate lunch there every day, as it was the only place in Paris where the tower was not visible. You can still eat there today.

La Dame de Fer is a circular yoke cardigan knit seamlessly from the top down. An attractive slip stitch pattern inspired by the ironwork of the Eiffel Tower adorns the yoke. With ¾ sleeves and worked in fingering weight yarn, you will reach for this cardigan year 'round.

SIZE

XS (S, M, L, 1X, 2X, 3X) to fit bust sizes 28 (32, 36, 40, 44, 48, 52) inches/71 (81, 91, 101, 111, 122, 132) cm, shown in size S with 2 inches/5 cm of positive ease

MATERIALS

Les Petits Points Parisiens Basique fingering (100% Superwash Merino; 437 yd/400 m per 100 g skein); Color: Abbesses; 3 (3, 3, 4, 4, 5) skeins or approximately 900 (1000, 1200, 1400, 1600, 1800) m of fingering yarn

US4/3.5 mm circular needle, 24-inch/60 cm for yoke, body, and sleeves (or size needed to achieve gauge)

US2/2.75 mm circular needle, 24-inch/60 cm for ribbing (or approximately 0.75 mm smaller than gauge needle)

Tapestry needle, stitch holders and waste yarn, stitch markers, 11–13 ½-inch/10 mm buttons

GAUGE

26 sts x 35 rows = 4 inches/10 cm with larger needle in Stockinette stitch, after blocking

26 sts x 38 rows = 4 inches/10 cm with larger needle in La Dame de Fer stitch, after blocking

Finished Measurements
Neck: 16¼ (16¾, 17¾, 18, 19½, 21½, 23¼) inches/40 (42, 44, 45, 49, 53, 58) cm
Bust: 31 (35, 37, 42, 47, 51, 56) inches/78 (90, 95, 108, 119, 130, 141) cm
Upper Arm: 11 (12¼, 13½, 14¾, 15¾, 17, 18¼) inches/28 (31, 34, 37, 39, 42, 45) cm
Wrist: 6¼ (6½, 7, 7½, 8, 8¼, 9) inches/17 (16, 18, 19, 20, 21, 22) cm
Body & Sleeve Length: 17 (17, 17, 17, 17, 17, 17) inches/43 (43, 43, 43, 43, 43, 43) cm from underarm

Les Petits Points Parisiens
Paris, France
lespetitspointsparisiens.com
@lespetitspointsparisiens

NECKBAND

With smaller needle, CO 105 (109, 115, 117, 127, 139, 151) sts.

Row 1 (RS): K1, (p1, k1) to end of row.

Row 2 (WS): (P1, k1) to last st, p1.

Repeat Rows 1&2 three more times.

YOKE

Change to larger needle.

1st inc row (RS): K36 (24, 21, 6, 2, 2, 2), work (k2, m1-L) 18 (32, 38, 54, 62, 68, 74) times across, knit to end of row—123 (141, 153, 171, 189, 207, 225) sts.

Row 1 (WS): P3 (2, 2, 3, 2, 3, 2), pl m, work Row 1 of La Dame de Fer pattern across to last 3 (2, 2, 3, 2, 3, 2) sts, pl m, p3 (2, 2, 3, 2, 3, 2).

Row 2 (RS): K3 (2, 2, 3, 2, 3, 2), work in patt to m k3 (2, 2, 3, 2, 1, 3).

Row 3 (WS): P3 (2, 2, 3, 2, 1, 3), work in patt to m, p3 (2, 2, 3, 2, 1, 3).

Row 4 (RS): K3 (2, 2, 3, 2, 3, 2), work in patt to m, k3 (2, 2, 3, 2, 1, 3).

Repeat Rows 3&4 for 10 (10, 10, 10, 14, 14, 14) more times following La Dame de Fer pattern and ending with patt row 8 (8, 8, 8, 16, 16, 16).

Next row (WS): Purl to end of row.

2nd inc row (RS): K2 (1, 1, 2, 1, 2, 1), (m1-L, k2) to last 3 (2, 2, 3, 2, 3, 2) sts, m1-L, k3 (2, 2, 3, 2, 3, 2)—183 (211, 229, 255, 283, 309, 337) sts.

Row 1 (WS): Purl to end of row.

Row 2 (RS): Knit to end of row.

Row 3 (WS): P3 (3, 2, 3, 3, 2, 2), work in patt to m, p3 (3, 2, 3, 3, 2, 2).

Row 4 (RS): K3 (3, 2, 3, 3, 2, 2), work in patt to m, k3 (3, 2, 3, 3, 2, 2).

Row 5 (WS): P3 (3, 2, 3, 3, 2, 2), work in patt to m, p3 (3, 2, 3, 3, 2, 2).

Row 6 (RS): K3 (3, 2, 3, 3, 2, 2), work in patt to m, k3 (3, 2, 3, 3, 2, 2).

Repeat Rows 5&6 for 10 (10, 10, 10, 14, 14, 14) more times following La Dame de Fer pattern and ending with patt row 8 (8, 8, 8, 16, 16, 16).

Next row (WS): Purl to end of row.

3rd inc row (RS): K3 (5, 5, 3, 5, 3, 5), (m1-L, k3) to last 3 (5, 5, 3, 5, 3, 5) sts, m1-L, k3 (5, 5, 3, 5, 3, 5)—243 (279, 303, 339, 375, 411, 447) sts.

Row 1 (WS): Purl to end of row.

Row 2 (RS): Knit to end of row.

Row 3 (WS): P3, work Row 1 of La Dame de Fer pattern across to last 3 sts, p3.

La Dame de Fer Chart

Chart Key

☐ = RS: Knit; WS: Purl

• = RS: Purl; WS: Knit

¥ = Slip stitch with yarn in front

A = Insert needle under 3 loose strands, then purl next stitch

☐ = Pattern repeat

La Dame de Fer Pattern

Row 1 (WS): P2, (p1, k3) to last 3 sts, p3.

Row 2 (RS): K3, (sl 3 wyif, k1) to last 2 sts, k2.

Rows 3–6: Repeat Rows 1&2 twice.

Row 7: Repeat Row 1.

Row 8: P2, (p2, insert needle under 3 loose strands, then purl next stitch, p1) to last 3 sts, p3.

Row 9: P1, k1, (k2, p1, k1) to last 3 sts, k2, p1.

Row 10: K1, sl 2 wyif, (sl 1 wyif, k1, sl 2 wyif), to last 2 sts, sl 1 wyif, k1.

Rows 11–14: Repeat Rows 9&10 twice.

Row 15: Repeat Row 9.

Row 16: K2, (insert needle under 3 loose strands, then knit next stitch, k3) to last 3 sts, k3.

Row 4 (RS): K3, work in patt to last 3 sts, k3.

Row 5 (WS): P3, work in patt to last 3 sts, p3.

Row 6 (RS): K3, work in patt to last 3 sts, k3.

Repeat Rows 5–6 10 (10, 10, 10, 14, 14, 14) more times following La Dame de Fer pattern and ending with patt row 8 (8, 8, 8, 16, 16, 16).

Next row (WS): Purl to end of row.

4th inc row (RS): K4, (m1-L, k4) to last 3 sts, m1-L, k3—303 (348, 378, 423, 468, 513, 558) sts.

Work even in Stockinette st until yoke measures 7 (7¾, 8¾, 8¾, 9½, 9½, 10¼) inches/18 (20, 22, 22, 24, 24, 26) cm from below neckband ribbing, ending with a WS row.

BODY

On the following row, you will divide for the body and sleeves by placing the sleeve sts on hold in order to continue working the body of the pullover separately.

Dividing row (RS): K46 (53, 57, 64, 72, 79, 87), pl next 60 (68, 76, 84, 90, 98, 106) sts on waste yarn, turn work, use the Knitted method to CO 8 sts, turn work once more with RS facing, k91 (106, 112, 127, 144, 159, 172), pl next 60 (68, 76, 84, 90, 98, 106) sts on waste yarn, turn work, use the Knitted method to CO 8 sts, turn work once more with RS facing, knit to end of row—199 (228, 242, 271, 304, 333, 362) sts.
Work even in Stockinette st until body measures 15¾ inches/40 cm from dividing row, or 1¼ inches/3 cm less than desired body length.

Lower edge ribbing
Change to smaller needle.
Row 1 (RS): K1 (0, 0, 1, 0, 1, 0), (p1, k1) to end of row.
Row 2 (WS): (P1, k1) to last 1 (0, 0, 1, 0, 1, 0) st, p1 (0, 0, 1, 0, 1, 0).
Repeat Rows 1&2 six more times.
Bind off loosely.

SLEEVES

With larger needle and RS facing, beginning at center of underarm, pick up and knit 4 sts from Knitted CO + 2 sts between the picked up sts and the ones on hold in order to avoid holes, k60 (68, 76, 84, 90, 98, 106) held sleeve sts, then pick up and knit 2 sts between the sts just worked and the sts CO at the underarm, pick up and knit 4 sts from Knitted CO at the underarm—72 (80, 88, 96, 102, 110, 118) sts. Join in the rnd and pl mBOR.
On the following two rnds, you will decrease to compensate for the additionally picked up sts and the sts CO at the underarm.
Rnd 1: K5, k2tog, knit to last 7 sts, k2tog, k2tog, k5—70 (78, 86, 94, 100, 108, 116) sts.
Rnd 2: K4, k2tog, knit to last 6 sts, k2tog, k2tog, k4—68 (76, 84, 92, 98, 106, 114) sts.
Work even in Stockinette st in the rnd for 2 inches/5 cm.
Dec rnd: K1, ssk, knit to last 3 sts, k2tog,

k1—66 (74, 82, 90, 96, 104, 112) sts.
Repeat Dec rnd 7 (9, 11, 13, 14, 16, 18) more times, every 17 (13, 11, 9, 8, 7, 6) rnds—52 (56, 60, 64, 68, 72, 76) sts.
Work even in Stockinette st in the rnd until piece measures 17¼ inches/44 cm or 1¼ inches/3 cm less than desired sleeve length.
Dec rnd: (K2, k2tog) to last 4 (0, 4, 0, 4, 0, 4) sts, k4 (0, 4, 0, 4, 0, 4)—40 (42, 46, 48, 52, 54, 58) sts.

Cuff ribbing
Change to smaller needle.
Rnd 1: (K1, p1) around.
Repeat this rnd thirteen more times.
Bind off loosely.

LEFT FRONT BAND

With smaller needle, RS facing, and beginning at top of left front, pick up and knit approximately 157 (163, 169, 169, 173, 173, 179) sts at a rate of about 3 out of 4 sts. This number may vary according to the desired garment length, but must remain an odd number.
Row 1 (WS): (P1, k1) to last st, p1.
Row 2 (RS): K1, (p1, k1) to end of row.
Repeat Rows 1&2 four more times, then Row

1 once more.
Bind off loosely.

RIGHT FRONT BAND

With smaller needle, RS facing, and beginning at bottom edge of right front, pick up and knit approximately 157 (163, 169, 169, 173, 173, 179) sts at a rate of about 3 out of 4 sts. If adjusting the number to accommodate a different garment length, ensure it is the same as for the left front band.
Row 1 (WS): (P1, k1) to last st, p1.
Row 2 (RS): K1, (p1, k1) to end of row.
Repeat Rows 1 and 2 once more.
Row 5 (WS): P1, k1, p1, k1, p1, (pl m, (k1, p1) 7 times) to last 12 (4, 10, 10, 0, 0, 6) sts, (k1, p1) to end of row.
Row 6 (one-row buttonholes, RS): ((K1, p1) to 2 sts before m, k2tog, yo, remove m) to last m, k1, p1, k1, p1, k1.
Rep Rows 1&2 twice more, then Row 1 once more.
Bind off loosely.

Finishing
Weave in loose ends. Block to finished measurements. Sew buttons to left front band, opposite buttonholes.

Escalier Hat & Cowl
by Sara Maternini/La Cave à Laine

Working jogless stripes

At the beginning of each round (but not when you transition from the mosaic pattern to stripes), you need to pay extra attention to work jogless stripes.

When you change from MC to CC (or from CC to MC), work the first round following instructions. When you arrive at the beginning of the second round of each color, use the right needle to lift the nearest half of the stitch below the first stitch of the left needle up on to the left needle. Knit these two stitches together, and continue to follow the pattern instructions.

Paris is filled with stairs, or **escaliers**, everywhere. The infinite stairs to ascend to Montmartre are only one example of how the city was built and functions. The mosaic motif in this hat and cowl set evokes the infinite stairs climbing to the incredible views of La Ville-Lumière.

If you have never tried mosaic knitting you are in for a treat: It's one of the nicest color knitting techniques, and you will master it in no time. As you will soon realize, tension does not matter so much in mosaic knitting as in other kinds of colorwork, so you can relax, following the rhythm of your needles.

SIZE

Hat: S (M, L) to fit head circumference of 21 (22, 24) inches/53 (56, 61) cm
Cowl: One Size

MATERIALS

La Bien Aimée Merino DK (100% Superwash Merino; 252 yd/230 m per 115 g skein)
Hat
  MC: Winter Garden; 1 skein or approximately 120 m of DK yarn
  CC: Winterfell; 1 skein or approximately 100 m of DK yarn
Cowl
  MC: Winter Garden; 2 skeins or approximately 380 m of DK yarn
  CC: Winterfell; 2 skeins or approximately 340 m of DK yarn
Hat
  US7/4.5 mm circular needle, 22-inch/55 cm (or size needed to achieve gauge)
  US6/4.0 mm (or approximately 0.5 mm smaller than gauge needle)
Cowl
  US7/4.5 mm circular needle, 37-inch/93 cm (or size needed to achieve gauge)
Stitch markers, tapestry needle

GAUGE

21 sts x 46 rnds = 4 inches/10 cm in Escalier Mosaic stitch on larger needles, after blocking

Finished Measurements

Hat: Circumference (at its largest point): 26 (27, 28¼) inches/66 (69, 72) cm, Length (longest side): 11½ inches/29 cm
Cowl: Circumference: 76 inches/190 cm, Depth: 13¾ inches/35 cm *Note: Stripes section will be significantly larger than mosaic section. Where the stripes have a depth of 13¾ inches/35cm, the mosaic has a depth of 9 inches/23cm.*

La Bien Aimée
Paris, France
labienaimee.com
@labienaimee

Chart Key

■ = CC

□ = MC

□ = Knit

V = Slip with yarn in back

□ = Pattern repeat

Escalier Mosaic Pattern

Work sts inside parentheses only for Hat

Rnd 1: With CC (k3, sl1, k1, sl1) to last 5 sts, k3, sl1, k1.

Rnd 2 and all even rnds: Repeat rnd just worked.

Rnd 3: With MC, k2, sl1, k3, (sl1, k1, sl1, k3) to last 5 sts, sl1, k1, sl1, k2.

Rnd 5: With CC, (k1, sl1, k3, sl1) to last 5 sts, k1, sl1, k3.

Rnd 7: With MC, (k2, sl1, k1, sl1, k1) to last 5 sts, k2, sl1, k2.

Rnd 9: With CC, (k1, sl1, k1, sl1, k2) to last 5 sts, k1, sl1, k1, sl1, k1.

Rnd 11: With MC, k4, sl1, k1, (sl1, k3, sl1, k1) to last 5 sts, sl1, k4.

COWL

With MC, CO 400 sts. Join in the rnd, being careful to not to twist, pl mBOR.

Rnd 1: (K1-tbl, p1) to end of rnd, placing another m after 203 sts from the BOR.

Work in established pattern for six rnds.

Knit three rnds.

Beginning from Rnd 1, work Escalier Mosaic Pattern to m, sl m, then knit to end of rnd.

Work in established patterns, working first section in Escalier Mosaic and second in stripes according to the color used for the mosaic rnd, for 72 rnds total.

Break MC, leaving an 8-inch/20 cm tail.

With CC, knit three rnds.

Rnd 1: (K1-tbl, p1) to end of rnd.

Repeat Rnd 1 for six more times.

Bind off as follows: K1, put the st back to the left needle, (k2tog-tbl, put st back on the left needle) to the end of rnd.

Break CC, leaving a 8-inch / 20 cm tail.

HAT

With smaller needles and MC, CO, with your favorite method, 80 (84, 90) sts. Join in the rnd, being careful to not to twist, pl mBOR.

Brim

Rnd 1: (K1-tbl, p1) to end of rnd.

Repeat Rnd 1 for 17 more times.

Repeat Rnd 1 once more, working as follows:

S size: (K1-tbl, p1) to end of rnd.

M size: M1-L, (K1-tbl, p1) to end of rnd—85 sts.

L size: (K1-tbl, p1) to end of rnd.

Next Round: (K5, m1-L) to the end of rnd—96 (102, 108) sts.

Change to larger needles and knit one rnd.

Beginning from Rnd 1, work sts in parentheses only (or only in the repeat section of the chart) of Escalier Mosaic Pattern to end of rnd.

Work in established pattern for 60 rnds total.

Break MC, leaving a 8-inch/20 cm tail.

With CC knit fourteen rnds.

Crown decreases

Rnd 1: (K4, k2tog) to end of rnd—80 (85, 90) sts.

Rnd 2 and all even rnds: Knit all sts.

Rnd 3: (K3, k2tog) to end of rnd—64 (68, 72) sts.

Rnd 5: (K2, k2tog) to end of rnd—48 (51, 54) sts.

Rnd 7: (K1, k2tog) to end of rnd—32 (34, 36) sts.

Rnd 9: K2tog to end of rnd—16 (17, 18) sts.

Break CC, leaving a 8-inch / 20 cm tail.

Use the tapestry needle to thread the tail through the remaining stitches, and pull to close the hat.

FINISHING

Weave in all ends. Gently wash cowl and hat. Block to finished measurements, stretching the mosaic part to fully open.

Sara loves Paris

What has your knitwear design journey been like?

I started modifying patterns little by little. I then decided to create something on my own, that would reflect my own personality and needs. I have always loved numbers and designing fulfils my need for structure.

Tell us a Paris story...

One night we got lost in the little streets of **Pigalle**, and it was magnificent! When in Paris, always try to leave the most touristy streets and wander in the small "ruelle" filled with history and hidden gardens. And look up, to the sky: look at the roofs!

Top Ten (movies, songs, books, tv shows)

1. All Fred Vargas detective stories 2. *Les Amants du Pont-Neuf* by Leos Carax 3. *Midnight in Paris* by Woody Allen 4. *L'élégance du hérisson* by Muriel Barbery 5. *Mon Oncle* by Jacques Tati
6. *Les Quatre cents coups* by Truffaut 7. *Jules et Jim* by Truffaut
8. *La Haine* by Matthieu Kassovitz 9. *Amélie* by Jean-Pierre Jeunet
10. *Caché* by Michael Haneke

Métro knitting: must-have or never ever? Favorite station?

Knitting always and every where, no matter what! All the art nouveau stations are my favorites.

Picker or thrower?

I am definitely a picker.

Project monogamy or cast on all the things?

I cast on all the time, all the things!

Favorite places to eat/drink/knit in Paris?

I have always had a weakness for all the Chinese shops and restaurants in **Avenue d'Ivry** in the 13°, as well as all the North African restaurants in the neighborhood of **La Goutte d'Or** in the 18°. A must try is one of the **Pierre Hermé** pastries, from macarons to chocolate—they have a boutique in almost every Arrondissement. But also try **Ladurée**: the 1862 art nouveau salon in the historic boutique on the **Rue Royal** is incredible! There are eight other Ladurées, too, scattered around Paris.

Jardin à la Française Socks
by Chloé Fourtune-Ravard/Tisserin Coquet

Working with two colors & color dominance

Stranded colorwork is created by knitting two colors in the same round: the background color and a pattern color. In this pattern, the MC is always the background color, and the CC is always the pattern color.

The yarn held lower will be slightly longer than the other one. This will make it more dominant. To allow the colorwork pattern to pop, the pattern color should always be the dominant one. If you're working with yarns held in both hands, the dominant color should be held in the left hand. If you're working with yarns held in the same hand, the dominant color should be held lower than the background color at all times.

Did you know that some of the most beautiful gardens of Paris were created back in the 17th century?

André Le Nôtre became the chief gardener of Louis XIV in 1645 which enabled him to create world-renowned gardens like the Gardens of the Tuileries Palace in the heart of Paris, the Château de Vaux-le-Vicomte and Château de Fontainebleau gardens, and the Gardens of Versailles.

The **Jardin à la Française** socks are a tribute to these gardens where I spent countless hours wandering. With their unexpected twists and turns, there is always something new to discover. The French formal gardens are designed with geometric and color rules to enhance perspective and symmetry as the vegetation contrasts with bright paths to create intricate parterres.

These socks are knitted from the cuff down, in an all-over geometric stranded colorwork stitch pattern based on the typical shapes and styles of French formal gardens. Their ribbing, reinforced heel flap, and toes are worked in the background color to mimic the plant-free garden entrances and alleyways and allow for a better fit and ease of wear.

SIZE

S (M, L), to fit foot circumferences of 7½–8¼ (8¼–9, 9–9¾) inches/19–21 (21–23, 23–25) cm

MATERIALS

(Vi)laines Chaussettes (75% Superwash Wool/25% Nylon; 437 yd/400 m per 100 g skein) or similar fingering yarn
MC: Jeter des perles aux cochons (Casting pearls before swine); 1 (1, 1) skein
CC: Sauter dans les fougères (Jumping in the ferns); 1 (1, 1) skein
US1.5/2.5 mm circular needle, 32-inch/80 cm (or size needed to achieve gauge)
Tapestry needle

GAUGE

32 sts x 44 rnds = 4 inches/10 cm in Stockinette stitch worked in the round, after blocking
36 sts x 43 rnds = 4 inches/10 cm in stranded colorwork pattern stitch worked in the round, after blocking.

Finished Measurements
Circumference: 7¼ (8, 8¾) inches/18.5 (20.5, 22.5) cm
Leg length: 5 (5 ¾, 6¼) inches/13 (14.5, 16) cm
Foot length, heel and toes included: 7 (7¾, 8¾) inches/18 (20, 22.5) cm
Toe length: 2 (2, 2½) inches/5 (5.5, 6.5) cm

(Vi)laines
Lyons, France
etsy.com/shop/Vilaines
@lainesvilaines

CUFF

With MC, CO 60 (68, 76) sts. Join to work in the rnd.

Rnd 1: (K1, p1) around.

Repeat Rnd 1 a total of 15 (17, 19) times.

LEG

Note: The first 29 (33, 37) sts will become the back of your sock, the next 31 (35, 39) will be the front.

Work the back sts following the Back charts (see p. 22) and the front sts following the Front charts (see p. 21) according to your size.

With MC, knit 1 (2, 3) rnds, then work Charts A for Back and Front according to your size.

With MC, knit 2 (4, 6) rnds, then work Charts B for Back and Front according your size.

With MC, knit 2 (4, 6) rnds, then work Charts C for Back and Front according your size.

With MC, knit 1 (2, 3) rnds.

HEEL FLAP

Note: Heel flap and turn will be working flat in MC only, across the back sts, i.e. the first 29 (33, 37) sts.

Row 1 (RS): (Sl1, k1) to last st, k1.

Row 2 (WS): Sl1, purl to end of row.

Repeat Rows 1–2 a total of 14 (16, 18) times, for a total of 28 (32, 36) rows.

Heel Turn

Note: The heel turn is worked in short rows.

Row 1 (RS): Sl1, k15 (17, 19), ssk, k1, turn.

Row 2 (WS): Sl1, p4, p2tog, p1, turn—10 (12, 14) sts on either side of the 7 (7, 7) central sts.

Row 3: Sl1, knit to 1 st before the gap, ssk over the gap, k1, turn.

Row 4: Sl1, purl to last st before the gap, p2tog over the gap, p1, turn.

Repeat Rows 3–4 a total of 5 (6, 7) times. All stitches each side have been worked—17 (19, 21) sts.

Cut MC, leaving a 6 inch/15 cm tail.

Gusset Decreases and Foot

Note: Your heel is now completed. You will now start to knit in the rnd again with both colors.

At the base of the heel flap, re-join MC, then pick-up and knit 1 st to prevent a gap forming, at the join between leg and heel on the side where you left your CC. This is your new beginning of rnd.

Pick-up and knit 14 (16, 18) stitches along the side edge of the heel flap (one in each slipped stitch)—32 (36, 40) sole sts.

Knit across all heel sts.

Pick up and knit 14 (16, 18) stitches along the side edge of the heel flap (one in each slipped stitch). Pick up one extra st between the heel and the instep to prevent a gap forming—78 (88, 98) sts including 47 (53, 59) sole sts.

Knit across all instep sts.

Work the sole sts following the Charts A for Sole (see p. 24) and Front (see p. 21) according to your size.

With MC, knit 2 (4, 6) rnds, then work Charts B for Sole (see p. 23) and Front (see p. 21) according your size.

With MC, knit 2 (4, 6) rnds, then work Charts C for Sole (see p. 23) and Front (see p. 21) according your size.

With MC, knit 1 (2, 3) rnds. Cut CC.

If necessary, add MC stockinette stitch rnds before starting the Toes to adjust the foot length to your foot measurements. Toes Section should begin 1¾ (2, 2¼) inches/4.5 (5, 5.5) cm before the desired foot length.

TOES

Note: Toes are worked in MC only.

Slide the first instep stitch to the sole.

Read the following definitions, then see below for instructions.

Dec Rnd: (K1, ssk, knit to last 3 sts, k2tog, k1) twice—4 sts dec'd.

Plain Rnd: Knit around.

Work (1 Dec Rnd, 1 Plain Rnd) 1 (1, 2) time(s)—56 (64, 68) sts.

Work (1 Dec Rnd, 4 Plain Rnds) 0 (1, 1) time(s)—56 (60, 64) sts.

Work (1 Dec Rnd, 3 Plain Rnds) 2 (1, 1) time(s)—48 (56, 60) sts.

Work (1 Dec Rnd, 2 Plain Rnds) 1 (1, 1) time—44 (52, 56) sts.

Work (1 Dec Rnd, 1 Plain Rnd) 3 (4, 4) times—32 (36, 40) sts.

Work Dec Rnd, 2 (3, 4) times—24 (24, 24) sts.

Finishing

Graft the remaining sts using Kitchener stitch (see p. 66). Knit the second sock. Weave in all ends. Wet block your socks trying to even the colorwork tension all around.

Front Chart C

With MC, knit 2 (4, 6) rnds, then work Front Chart C according to your size.

Front Chart B

With MC, knit 2 (4, 6) rnds, then work Front Chart B according to your size.

Front Chart A

With MC, knit 1 (2, 3) rnds, then work Front Chart A according to your size.

Chart Key

☐ = Knit with color indicated

☒ = Ssk

☒ = K2tog

⊞ = Pick up and knit

☐ = Center Motif

☐ = Additional stitches for Sizes S, M, L

Color Legend

■ = CC

☐ = MC

Back Chart C

With MC, knit 2 (4, 6) rnds, then work Back Chart C according to your size.

Back Chart B

With MC, knit 2 (4, 6) rnds, then work Back Chart B according to your size.

Back Chart A

With MC, knit 1 (2, 3) rnds, then work Back Chart A according to your size.

Chart Key

- ☐ = Knit with color indicated
- ⧹ = Ssk
- ⧸ = K2tog
- + = Pick up and knit
- ☐ = Center Motif
- ☐ = Additional stitches for Sizes S, M, L

Color Legend

- ▩ = CC
- ☐ = MC

Short Row Heel Turn

Your heel turn will be worked through short rows. At the end of each short row, you will turn your work and continue knitting on the other side of the work, slipping the first stitch of each row. This will create a gap between worked and un-worked stitches on either side of the heel.

The pattern sizes are designed to match classic 56 (64, 72) sock sizes, taking into account a tighter gauge than usual because of the colorwork. Choose your size and needles according to your usual ones.

If your foot length is shorter than the minimum foot length of your size of choice, you can remove background color rnds to adapt the colorwork pattern length to your needs.

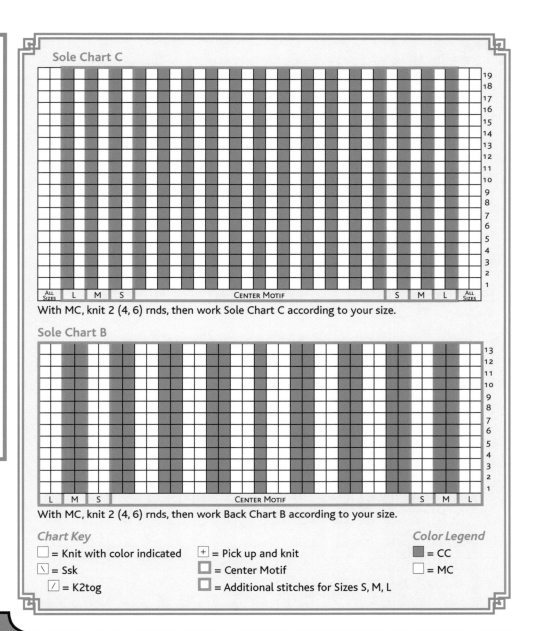

Sole Chart C

With MC, knit 2 (4, 6) rnds, then work Sole Chart C according to your size.

Sole Chart B

With MC, knit 2 (4, 6) rnds, then work Back Chart B according to your size.

Chart Key

- □ = Knit with color indicated
- \ = Ssk
- / = K2tog
- + = Pick up and knit
- □ = Center Motif
- □ = Additional stitches for Sizes S, M, L

Color Legend

- ■ = CC
- □ = MC

Chloé loves Paris

What has your knitwear design journey been like?

I have always loved reinterpreting patterns to truly make them my own. One day at lunch with a yarn shop owner friend of mine, while talking about yarns and colorways, she showed me some new hand painted fingering yarn. She loved the yarn but had no idea how to showcase it. All I could see was a pair of socks. She trusted me enough to create and write the *Premier Flocon* sock pattern with it, my very first knitting pattern, and that's how it all started.

Métro knitting: must-have or never ever?
Favorite station?

Must-have! **Bastille**, its pretty walls and lovely neighborhood is my actual favorite, but for many years it has been **Rambuteau** because getting in this station meant I was finally able to go home after a whole day spent studying in the library.

Favorite neighborhood?

The historical center of Paris is my all-time favorite, you always have something new to uncover, but the 14° is growing on me.

Picker or thrower?
Project monogamy or cast on all the things?

Mainly thrower but I use both hands and techniques while working stranded colorwork or brioche. Lately I'm kind of monogamy-ish: I like to have different kind of WIPs depending of the occasion but only one of the same kind (knit night, Métro knitting, etc.)

Favorite places to eat/drink/knit in Paris?

I really enjoy the parks (like the **Jardins du Luxembourg** and the **Parc de Bercy**) and the **Seine banks**—a quiet place in the heart of the city. **Lemon in Paris** in the 2° is a small Icelandic juice bar with amazing smoothies. **Le Paradis du Fruit** with eight locations around Paris has great salads. **Chez Michel** on the Butte aux cailles in the 13° has a large selection of beers and rums, as do lots of other bars in the area.

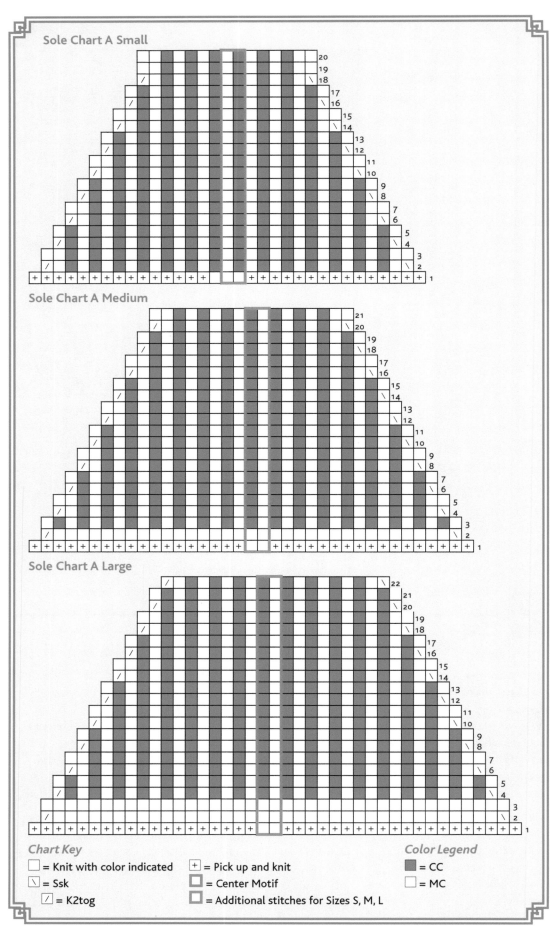

Sole Chart A Small

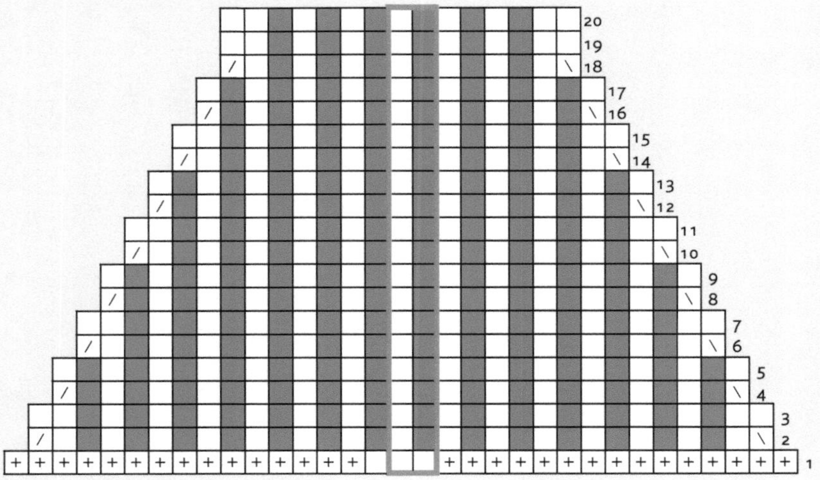

Sole Chart A Medium

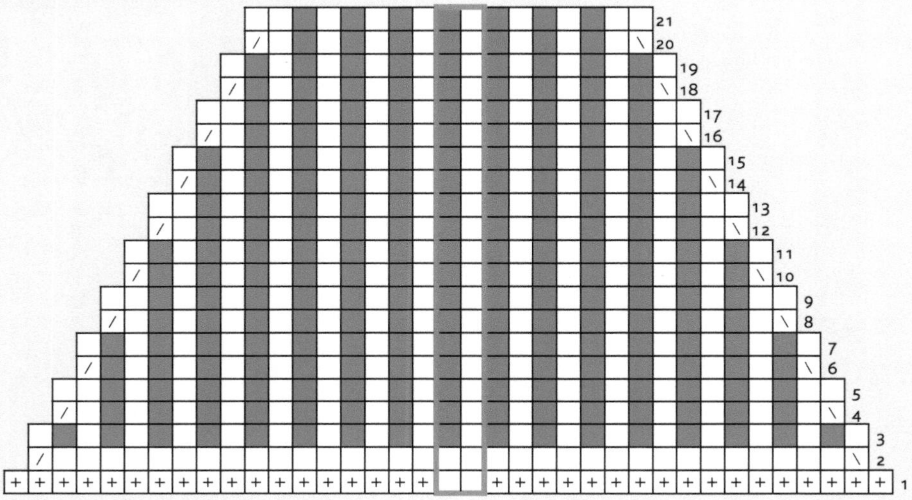

Sole Chart A Large

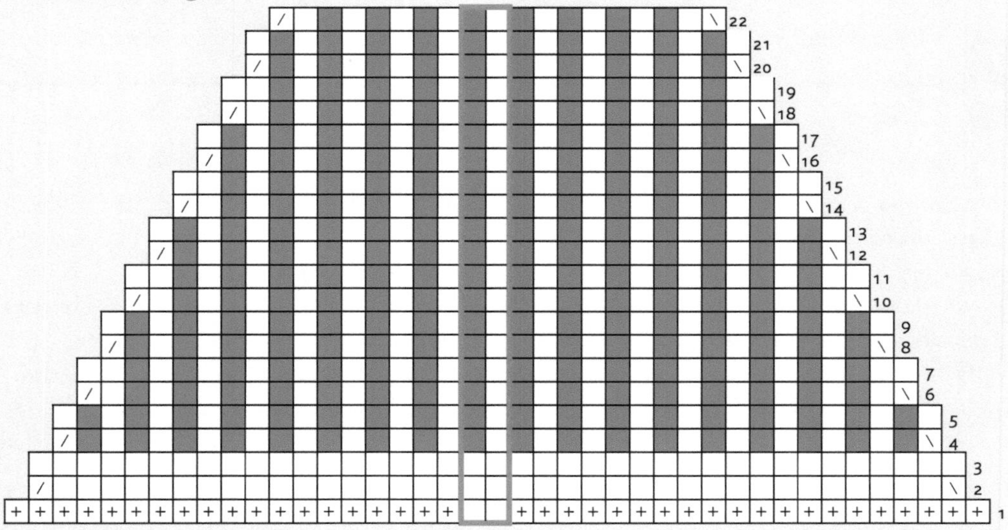

Chart Key

- ☐ = Knit with color indicated
- \ = Ssk
- / = K2tog
- + = Pick up and knit
- ☐ = Center Motif
- ☐ = Additional stitches for Sizes S, M, L

Color Legend

- ■ = CC
- ☐ = MC

Kathleen loves Paris

Top Ten (movies, songs, books, tv shows)

La belle et la bête directed by Jean Cocteau with Josette Day and Jean Marais—swoon-worthy French film

My Life in France by Julia Child—Julia + France = Perfection

Audrey Hepburn's Paris movies: *Sabrina, Funny Face, Love in the Afternoon, How to Steal a Million*—she was such *la gamine*

Paris to the Moon by Adam Gopnik—a New Yorker in Paris

Madeline by Ludwig Bemelmans—classic children's book

For Scent-imental Reasons from Looney Tunes with Pepé Le Pew and Penelope Pussycat—so un-PC, yet I love it: *Sacré cerise!*

Le Divorce by Diane Johnson—modern coming-of-age in Paris

"French accordion music," as my family calls it

Absolutely Fabulous episodes "France" and "Paris"—Edina, Patsy, Saffron, and Bubble's absurd moments on a vineyard vacation and then at a Parisian fashion shoot, both hilarious

Me Talk Pretty One Day by David Sedaris—learning French in Paris was never so funny

Métro knitting: must-have or never ever?

I'm too busy checking out all the Parisians—saw a gentleman in a gorgeous knitted tie once—to find time to knit on the Métro.

Picker or thrower?

Project monogamy or cast on all the things?

Thrower, though I can pick when doing colorwork. Monogamy for me because I really love completing a project so prefer to focus on one thing at a time.

Favorite places to eat/drink/knit in Paris?

- Staying in the 14° on our most recent visit, we discovered **Café Daguerre** on our first morning and went back every day for the best *café au lait* and *petit dejeuner* (with knitting).
- Climbing to the first level of the **Eiffel Tower** in the 7°, then eating *macarons* (picked up at **Ladurée Paris Bonaparte** in the 6°) and knitting. When you walk everywhere (and climb the stairs), you can eat whatever you like!

- Nothing is better than watching the sun set over **Notre-Dame** while eating *escargots en croute* and drinking *rosé* outside at **Le Petit Châtelet** in the 5°. After *profiteroles* or flaming *crêpes Suzette*, saunter next door to **Shakespeare & Co.** for the best English bookshop in Paris (less crowded after dinner). Stop by **Odette Paris** before dinner for one of their famous *choux à la crème* (and a glass of champagne).
- More *rosé*, this time with *crêpes aux marrons glacés* in the afternoon under an umbrella at the **Tuileries** in the 1° (the **Louvre** and **Palais Royal** are nearby). The upside to jetlag: eat and drink whatever strikes your fancy at any time of day.
- Our loveliest meal was at **Le Bistrot des Campagnes** in the 14°, a cozy, friendly spot with a constantly updated *prix fixe* menu— everything is fresh, in season, and delicious, for vegetarian, pescatarian, or carnivore.
- If you can, be sure to visit an outdoor *marché*. The organic produce at the **Marché Raspail** in the 6° on Sunday was gorgeous. I found some lovely souvenirs (a wee, carved wooden scoop and some *sel de bain*). From there you should walk up Rue de Rennes to **Café de Flore** or **Les Deux Magots**, both classics.

Marinière Hat & Mitts
by Lucile Francomme/Lucile Ateliers Designs

Ahoy! Here is a set of hat and mitts which smell of the stimulating sea air.

You probably know the famous "**marinière**" which inspired these patterns. The mariniere is the official uniform of the French Navy seaman, but since Coco Chanel was inspired by it, blue stripes have become an essential part of our wardrobes. As accessories, stripes are the graphic touch all sober outfits need.

Sailor men, **matelots** in French, wore a precise number of indigo blue stripes. The rule is blue stripes have to be two times thinner than white stripes, which you will find here. I also wanted to think of stripes in a different way, so chose to work with a light color with speckles. They are particularly delicate so as not to melt the solid color line. I love the effect, it adds a touch of modernity and reminds me

of the spray of the sea, just to let us sail a little round after round.

Knitting stripes is a pleasure as much for the result as for the practice. They are very attractive and punctuate the work so well that you will never get bored. The construction of each project is classic. As they are worked in the round, I suggest you make the stripes with a special technique to minimize the inevitable jog at the beginning of the round. You can use this on every striped knitting project you work on. Mitts are worked from the cuff to the fingers, increasing on one side for the thumb. Hat is worked from the brim to the top. Both fit well, thanks to the garter stitch border and stockinette stitch we find on each project.

Welcome aboard for these great little knits, and join the timeless navy style!

SIZE

Hat: S (M, L) to fit head circumference of 19½ (21½, 23) inches/49.5 (54.5, 58.5) cm

Mitts: S (M, L) to fit hand circumference of 6 (6½, 7) inches/15 (16.5, 18) cm

MATERIALS

Tôt Le Matin TOT SOCK 100% (100% Superwash Merino; 436 yd/400 m per 100 g skein) or similar fingering yarn

Hat
  MC: Amelie; 1 (1, 1) skein or approximately 124 (137, 151) m
  CC: Dark; 1 (1, 1) skein or approximately 48 (54, 59) m

Mitts
  MC: Amelie; 1 (1, 1) skein or approximately 80 (88, 97) m
  CC: Dark; 1 (1, 1) skein or approximately 48 (54, 59) m

US3/3.25 mm circular needle, 24-inch/60 cm (or size needed to achieve gauge)

US2.5/3.0 mm circular needle, 24-inch/60 cm (or approximately 0.5 mm smaller than gauge needle)

Tapestry needle, stitch markers, waste yarn for holding thumb stitches

GAUGE

29 sts x 41 rnds = 4 inches/10 cm in the rnd in Stockinette stitch with larger needles, after blocking

Finished Measurements
Hat: To fit head circumference of 19½ (21½, 23) inches/49.5 (54.5, 58.5) cm when stretched, Length: 9¼ inches/23.5 cm
Mitts: Hand Circumference: 6 (6½, 7) inches/15 (16.5, 18) cm

Tôt Le Matin
Saint-Georges-Motel, France
tot-le-matin.com
@tot_le_matin_yarns

Jogless stripes in the round in garter stitch

To minimize the visible jog at the beginning of the round, follow these steps every time you change color:

1st Round: Wrap the first stitch with the last color from back to front, from left to right. Work all stitches (included the first one wrapped) with the new color.

Jogless stripes in the round in stockinette stitch

1st Round: The new thread goes over the previous one, work the first stitch loosely, work all the other stitches as usual.

2nd Round: Slip the first stitch purlwise, work all the other stitches as usual.

In the case of a stripe with only one round: Work the first round as described with the new color, work the 2nd one with the new color and proceed as usual.

German Short Rows

This pattern includes short rows thanks to which all the fingers of the hand will be properly covered.

Step 1: Work to the point where the pattern asks you to make one German Short Row.

Step 2: Move the yarn to the other side of the work—not in front of the needle, but over it. The stitch is now a two strand stitch and counts as one stitch. Then follow pattern instructions.

Lace Bind-Off

Step 1: Knit two stitches together through the back loop.

Step 2: Slip the stitch on the right needle back to the left needle.

Repeat Steps 1&2.

HAT

Hat border

With smaller needles and MC, CO 128 (136, 144) sts. Join in the rnd being careful not to twist your stitches and pl mBOR.

Rnd 1: Using MC, purl all sts.

Rnd 2: Wrap the 1st st with MC, then using CC, knit all sts.

Rnd 3: Using CC, purl all sts.

Rnd 4: Wrap the 1st st with CC, then using MC, knit all sts.

Repeat Rnds 2–4 twice more.

Repeat Rnd 1 once more.

Hat body

Change to larger needles.

Rnds 1–2: Using CC, knit all sts.

Rnds 3–6: Using MC, knit all sts.

Repeat Rnds 1–6 a total of 7 (6, 5) times.

At the same time, on last row: Pl m every 16 (17, 18) sts.

Hat decreases

Size L only:

Rnds 1–2: Using CC, knit all sts.

Rnds 3–4: Using MC, knit all sts.

Rnd 5: Using MC, (knit to 2 sts before m, ssk, sl m) to end of rnd—8 sts dec'd.

Rnd 6: Using MC, knit all sts—136 sts.

Sizes M, L only:

Rnds 1–2: Using CC, knit all sts.

Rnds 3–4: Using MC, knit all sts.

Rnd 5: Using MC, (knit to 2 sts before m, ssk, sl m) to end of rnd—8 sts dec'd.

Rnd 6: Using MC, knit all sts—128 sts for both sizes.

All sizes:

Rnd 1: Using CC, knit all sts.

Rnd 2: Using CC, (knit to 2 sts before m, k2tog, sl m) to end of rnd—8 sts dec'd.

Rnds 3–4: Using MC, knit all sts.

Rnd 5: Using MC, (knit to 2 sts before m, k2tog, sl m) to end of rnd—8 sts dec'd.

Rnd 6: Using MC, knit all sts.

Repeat Rnds 1–6 a total of 3 times—80 sts for all sizes.

End of hat

Rnd 19: Using CC, knit all sts.

Rnd 20: Using MC, (knit to 2 sts before m, k2tog, sl m) to end of rnd—8 sts dec'd.

Rnds 21–22: Using MC, knit all sts.

Rnd 23: Using MC, (knit to 2 sts before m, k2tog, sl m) to end of rnd—8 sts dec'd.

Rnd 24: Using MC, knit all sts.
Repeat Rounds 23–24 a total of 6 times—24 sts for all sizes.

Finishing

Break yarn, thread onto tapestry needle, pull needle through remaining live sts, and pull tight to secure top. Turning work inside out, weave in all ends. Block gently.

MITTS (Make Two)

Cuff

With smaller needles and MC, CO 44 (48, 56) sts. Join for working in the rnd being careful not to twist your stitches and pl mBOR.
Rnd 1: Using MC, purl all sts.
Rnd 2: Wrap the 1st st with MC, then using CC, knit all sts.
Rnd 3: Using CC purl all sts.
Rnd 4: Wrap the 1st st with CC, then using MC, knit all sts.
Repeat Rounds 2–4 twice more.
Repeat Rnd 1 once more.

Hand

Change to larger needles.
Rnds 1–2: Using CC, knit all sts.
Rnds 3–6: Using MC, knit all sts.
At the same time, on last row: Pl m after the 21st (23rd, 26th) st and one after the 23rd (25th, 30th) st.

Thumb increases

Rnd 1: Using CC, knit all sts.
Rnd 2 (inc): Using CC, knit to m, sl m, m1-L, knit to m, m1-R, sl m, knit to end—2 sts inc'd.
Rounds 3–4: Using MC, knit all sts.
Rnd 5 (inc): Using MC, knit to m, sl m, m1-L, knit to m, m1-R, sl m, knit to end—2 sts inc'd.
Rnd 6: Using MC, knit all sts.
Repeat Rounds 1–6 three more times—60 (64, 72) sts.

Hand increases

Rnd 1: Using CC, knit all sts.
Rnd 2 (inc): Using CC, knit to m, m1-R, sl m, knit to m, sl m, m1-L, knit to end—62 (66, 74) sts.
Rounds 3–4: Using MC, knit all sts.
Rnd 5 (inc): Using MC, knit to m, m1-R, sl m, knit to m, sl m, m1-L, knit to end—64 (68, 76) sts.
Rnd 6: Using MC, knit all sts.

Separating thumb and hand

Rnd 1: Using CC, k23 (25, 28), remove m, place the next 18 (18, 20) sts on waste yarn, CO 4 sts, remove m, knit to end—50 (54, 60) sts for the hand, 18 (18, 20) sts held for the thumb.

Top of hand

Rnd 1: Using CC, knit all sts.
Rnds 2–5: Using MC, knit all sts.
Rnds 6–7: Using CC, knit all sts.
Rnds 8–11: Using MC, knit all sts.
Rnd 12: Using CC, knit all sts.
Rnds 13–15: Using MC, knit all sts.

German short rows:

Rnd 16 (RS): Using MC, k42 (46, 52), 1 German Short Row (see p. 28) on next st.
Rnd 17 (WS): Turn work and sl short row st, p28 (32, 38), 1 German Short Row on next st.
Rnd 18: Turn work and sl short row st, k22 (26, 32), 1 German Short Row on next st.
Rnd 19: Turn work and sl short row st, p16 (22, 28), 1 German Short Row on next st.
Rnd 20: Turn work and sl short row st, knit all sts.

Top of hand

Change to smaller needles.
Rnd 21: Using MC, purl all sts.
Rnd 22: Wrap the 1st st with MC, then using CC, knit all sts.
Rnd 23: Using CC, purl all sts.
Rnd 24: Wrap the 1st st with CC, then using MC, knit all sts.
Rnd 25: Using MC, purl all sts.
Bind off all sts with Lace Bind-Off method (see p. 28).

Thumb

Put the 18 (18, 20) thumb sts on the larger needles.
With CC, starting from the middle of the 4 cast on sts, pick up 2 sts in each 2 sts cast on for the hand, pick up 1 additional st before thumb to close the hole, knit all thumb sts, pick up 1 additional st in the hand part, then pick up 2 sts in each CO st—24 (24, 26) sts.
Rnd 1 (dec): Using CC, k2tog, knit to last 2 sts, ssk—22 (22, 24) sts.
Rnds 2–5: Using MC, knit all sts.
Rnd 6: Using CC, knit all sts.
Rnds 7–10: Using MC, knit all sts.

Top of thumb

Change to smaller needles.
Rnd 11: Using MC, purl all sts.
Rnd 12: Wrap the 1st st with MC, then using CC, knit all sts.
Rnd 13: Using CC, purl all sts.
Rnd 14: Wrap the 1st st with CC, then using MC, knit all sts.
Rnd 15: Using MC, purl all sts.
Bind off all sts with Lace Bind-Off method.

Finishing

Weave in all ends. Block gently.

What has your knitwear design journey been like?

It starts with an idea that comes to me like a flash, often inspired by the wool I have or colors. I refine this idea by sketching until I have something I like. As I draw, I note some technical elements: construction, texture, ease... Then comes the moment of the sample, when I can begin to see the project and also to start the calculations! Everything happens on the computer: I can enter formulas to make my corrections quickly and have a clean overview of my work. I finally write a general plan of written explanations and use all of this to knit the prototype. Correct. Knit again. Unravel. Knit again... Until I like it!

Top Ten

Theater: *Phèdre*, Racine
Music: all Arcade Fire
Book: *Voyage au bout de la nuit* by Louis-Ferdinand Céline
Series: *Community*
Video game: Tomb Raider I to V
Movie: *Moonrise Kingdom*
Humor: *Les Nuls*
Painting: Impressionnisme
Strip cartoon: *Notes, Boulet*
TV show: *Secrets d'Histoire*

Tell us a Paris story...

As everyone knows, Paris is the city of love. I do not really believe what people say, but I have to be honest: It worked for me, too! I met my fiancé Paul here, and our first date was a little adventure. We went to a concert in the 11°. I do not remember anything other than the pleasant surprise that I had discovered a nice guy who knew how to ask questions but also had answers for me. We strolled from bars to restaurants, taking random streets. Every place we paused started a new discussion. We walked a lot. We talked and laughed, too. It was as if we had lived ten days together in just a few hours. Since that evening of November 2015, we have not left each other!

Métro knitting: must-have or never ever?

To take the Métro I have two obligations: take a ticket and take my knitting!

Favorite station?

The station I like most is **Arts et Métiers** station because the walls are covered with copper. It's like being in the Nautilus.

Project monogamy or cast on all the things?

I prefer to cast-on one project at a time. The more things I have to do, the more anxious I feel. The more I feel anxious, the tighter I knit—not good for gauge!

Favorite places to eat/drink/knit in Paris?

Favorite place to eat : **Chez Gladines** in the 13° and their Basque specialties.
Favorite place to drink : Along the banks of the **Seine**.
Favorite place to knit : At home!

Entrée de Fournisseurs
8, rue des FrancsBourgeois, 4° Arr. • Tél: +33 1 48 87 58 98
Website: lamercerieparisienne.com • Instagram: @ lamercerieparisienne

Enter through a beautiful little courtyard to visit this charming, authentic *mercerie* in the Marais. La Mercerie is the quintessential "old school" notions shop. Cards of buttons (prices on back, those with an X are out of stock), ribbons galore, Liberty of London fabric, and lots of yarns for *bébé* like Plassard, DMC, and Debbie Bliss. The staff are helpful but not overly friendly; you will need their assistance in cutting ribbon or fabric. Your various treasures will be placed in glassine envelopes ink-stamped with the shop name.

If you are on the search for parfum *and other French potions, the area around Entrée de Fournisseurs is for you: Editions de Parfums Frederic Malle, Diptyque, Caudalie, and more have storefronts nearby. Though closed the day we were there, we plan to visit Parfumerie Marie Antoinette next time. Sadly for us, lunch at Le loir dans la théiere was problematic (they were not happy to have a table full of knitters), but we did discover La mouette rieuse, a nearby bookshop with a café in the back (plus tables in a little courtyard) that we liked, with books in English and French, as well as a nice selection of notebooks (Tiger Paper, Leuchtterm) and gifts.*

Notre-Dame Shawl
by Christelle Bagéa/Tricot et Stitch

The Cathedral of Notre-Dame, on the Ile de la Cité in the center of Paris, was built between 1163 and 1345. This awe-inspiring monument, mainly in the gothic style, is a symbol of both medieval Paris and the Paris we know today, creating a bond across time and bearing testimony to the history of the city. This monument has always inspired creativity, be it in writing, painting, film. Knitting is no exception. The striking design of the south rose window, the cathedral's largest, given to the people by King Saint-Louis (also known as Louis IX) inspired this design.

Notre-Dame is knit in the round. It grows very fast in the beginning, thanks to the traditional pi-shawl construction detailed by Elizabeth Zimmermann in **Knitter's Almanac**.

Soon the rhythm of increases changes and, as the rounds get longer, you will find yourself working peacefully, slowly building the rose window and your own heirloom out of basic crossed stitches and simple lace, with just enough interest to make for thoroughly enjoyable TV knitting.

For this design, I had the pleasure to work with Maison Corlène, a French dyeing company specializing in quality yarns using natural dyeing techniques. I wanted a yarn and color that would highlight both texture and lace, and Aurore and Guillaume offered a brand new colorway in their high twist merino/silk blend: Anna May. It was the perfect match, a lovely neutral with a delicate pink undertone, just like the early morning sun reflecting on the stones of Notre-Dame. The silk

gives it shine and drape, perfect for lace (and blocking), while the high-twist highlights the crossed stitches. The yarn is a treat to work with and perfect for close-to-skin wearing.

Once finished, the best is yet to come: pi-shawls are endlessly versatile. Wrap it around you like a blanket, fold it in half and wear it as a regular half-pi shawl, or even as an extra-warm kerchief. It's a comforting yet practical garment that will soon become a wardrobe staple.

SIZE
One size

MATERIALS
Maison Corlène Belle Époque—mérinos soie high twist (80% Superwash Merino, 20% silk; 399 yd/365 m per 100 g skein); color: Anna May; 4 skeins or approximately 1320 m of fingering yarn

US6/4.0 mm interchangeable circular needle with 16, 24, 32, 40, 48, 60-inch/40, 60, 80, 100, 120, 150 cm cables and 4-inch/11 cm and (optional) 3-inch/8 cm needle points (or size needed to achieve gauge)

US6/4.0 mm crochet hook (to cast on)

Cable needle, tapestry needle, 11 stitch markers, 1 BOR stitch marker

GAUGE
22 sts x 32 rows = 4 inches/10 cm in Stockinette stitch, after blocking

Maison Corlène
Alsace, France
etsy.com/fr/shop/Maisoncorlene
@maisoncorlene

Finished Measurements
Diameter: 51 inches/130 cm

Chart 3 (see pp. 36–37)—708 sts, and Chart 4 (see pp. 36–37)—972 sts, by repeating each 12 times around, sl ms as you come to them, until Rnd 120 is complete.

BORDER

Rounds 121–131 will be worked by changing knitting direction on each rnd, thereby wrapping the first st of the following rnd and turning the work, in order to avoid purling long rnds. On the last st of each rnd, pick up the wrap and knit it together with the st, then wrap the first st of the next rnd and turn. Slide m as you go.

At the end of Rnd 120, wrap the first stitch of Rnd 121 and turn to work in the other direction.

Rnd 121 (WS): (K1, kfb, knit until 1 st remains before next m, kfb, k1, sl m) around—996 sts. W&T.

Rnd 122 (RS): (Yo, k2tog) around, moving m by one st when necessary and knitting the last k2tog as a k3tog with the wrap. W&T.

Rnd 123: Knit around. W&T.

Rnd 124: Same as Rnd 121—1,020 sts.

Rnds 125&126: Knit around. W&T.

Rnd 127: Same as Rnd 121—1,044 sts.

Rnds 128&129: Knit around. W&T.

Rnd 130: (K1, yo (k2tog, yo) until one st remains before m, k1, yo) around—1,068 sts. W&T.

Rnd 131: Knit around. W&T.

From Rnd 132 on, resume normal circular knitting.

Rnd 132: (K1-tbl, p1) around. Upon reaching the last stitch of the rnd, pick up the wrap and knit it together with the st. Do not W&T.

Rnd 133: (M2, (k1-tbl, p1) to next m) around—1,092 sts.

Rounds 134–136: (K1-tbl, p1) around. Bind off very loosely using Jeny's Surprisingly Stretchy Bind-Off (see p. 66).

Finishing

Weave in all ends but do not trim them yet. Soak your shawl in lukewarm water with a drop of rinse-free wool wash. Squeeze out excess water gently and wrap it in a towel. Step on towel to remove a maximum of water. Block your shawl to finished measurements, pinning the center first and aligning the radius. Then pin each border point and each lace point, without excessively stretching. Once dry, unpin your shawl and trim all ends.

CENTER

With 32 inch/80 cm cable and 4 inch/11 cm needle points, CO12 sts using Emily Ocker's Circular Beginning (see p. 66) and work in the rnd using the Magic Loop technique.

As soon as your shawl is big enough, switch to 16 inch/40 cm cable (using 3 inch/8 cm needle points) or to 24 inch/60 cm cable, to work in the rnd. As your shawl grows, you will have to increase the length of your cable up until the 60 inch/150 cm cable, which will be long enough to hold all your sts until bind off.

Rnd 1: Knit around.

Rnd 2: (Yo, k1) around—24 sts.

Rnd 3: (K1-tbl, k1) around.

Rnds 4–5: Knit around.

Rnd 6: (Yo, k1) around—48 sts.

Rnd 7: (K1-tbl, k1) around.

Rnds 8–11: Knit around.

Rnd 12: Purl around.

Rnd 13: (Yo, k1) around—96 sts.

Rnd 14: Purl around.

Rnd 15: Pl mBOR, k4, yo, k4, (pl m, k4, yo, k4) around—108 sts.

Continue knitting from Chart 1 (see p. 36)—300 sts, Chart 2 (see p. 36)—420 sts,

Christelle loves Paris

What has your knitwear design journey been like?

Three years ago, I was struck by a particular color combination: a beautiful black yarn on a sparkle base lay close to a few MadTosh unicorn tails I had just bought—so lovely! I browsed Ravelry for a pattern ... and amongst thousands, I could not find one to my taste for this particular yarn-y association. So I thought and thought ... and created my own pattern, the **Audrey** shawl (free on Ravelry). I took so much pleasure in designing and publishing it that I kept on going. The design bug had bitten. I've never stopped since!

Tell us a Paris story...

A few years ago, I worked for a company located on the **Champs-Élysées**, at the foot of the **Arc de Triomphe**. Each morning I would commute on line 2, of which a few stations are above ground. On days when the weather was beautiful, I would see the early morning sun reflecting on **Montmartre**, painting it pink. Or the Champs-Élysées, bathed in sunlight and unfolding before me in all their glory. I feel privileged to have had the opportunity to witness such breathtaking views of Paris, as part of my daily commute!

Top Ten Movies

1. *Star Wars* original trilogy 2. *Harry Potter* series 3. *Indiana Jones* saga 4. *Kingsman* 1 & 2 5. *Ghostbusters* (the first one) 6. *Die Hard* 1-2-3 7. *Lord of the Rings* trilogy 8. *The Hobbit* trilogy 9. *Love Actually* 10. *Alien* 1 & 2

Top Ten Songs

I've loved Prince's music since I was 14. My top ten songs are all by him.

1. *Anna Stesia* 2. *Purple Rain* 3. *Baby I'm a Star* 4. *The Sacrifice of Victor* 5. *Race* 6. *Alphabet Street* 7. *Starfish and Coffee* 8. *1999* 9. *Housequake* 10. *Kiss*

Top Ten Books

I love reading all the books in a saga.

1. *Jane Eyre* by Charlotte Brontë 2. *Harry Potter* saga by JK Rowling 3. All books by Fred Vargas 4. *The Ocean at the End of the Lane* by Neil Gaiman 5. *The Graveyard Book* by Neil Gaiman 6. *14* by Peter Clines 7. *We are Bob* saga by Dennis E. Taylor 8. *Outlander* saga by Diana Gabaldon 9. *Peter Grant* saga by Ben Aaronovitch 10. *The Martian* by Andy Weir

Top Ten TV shows

1. *The Walking Dead* 2. *Poldark* 3. *Game of Thrones* 4. *The Terror* 5. *Sherlock* 6. *Ripper Street* 7. *Shetland* 8. *Black Mirror* 9. *Outlander* 10. *Trapped*

Métro knitting: must-have or never ever? Favorite station?

When one can sit, a must-have! **Republique**.

Favorite places to eat/drink/knit in Paris?

The Starbucks on boulevard Poissonière in the 2°. I love the "English" style **Parc Monceau** in the 8° with its informal layout.

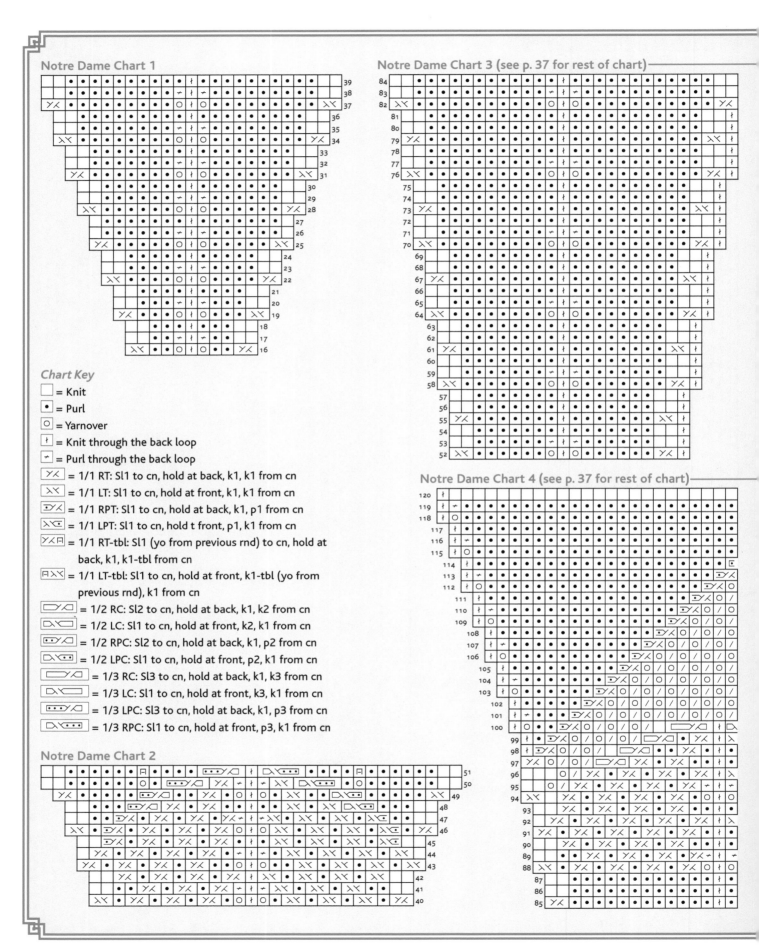

Notre Dame Chart 1

Notre Dame Chart 3 (see p. 37 for rest of chart)

Chart Key

☐ = Knit

• = Purl

O = Yarnover

↑ = Knit through the back loop

↜ = Purl through the back loop

⤫ = 1/1 RT: Sl1 to cn, hold at back, k1, k1 from cn

⤬ = 1/1 LT: Sl1 to cn, hold at front, k1, k1 from cn

⤫ = 1/1 RPT: Sl1 to cn, hold at back, k1, p1 from cn

⤬ = 1/1 LPT: Sl1 to cn, hold t front, p1, k1 from cn

⤫ = 1/1 RT-tbl: Sl1 (yo from previous rnd) to cn, hold at
back, k1, k1-tbl from cn

⤬ = 1/1 LT-tbl: Sl1 to cn, hold at front, k1-tbl (yo from
previous rnd), k1 from cn

⬭⤫ = 1/2 RC: Sl2 to cn, hold at back, k1, k2 from cn

⤬⬭ = 1/2 LC: Sl1 to cn, hold at front, k2, k1 from cn

⬭⤫ = 1/2 RPC: Sl2 to cn, hold at back, k1, p2 from cn

⤬⬭ = 1/2 LPC: Sl1 to cn, hold at front, p2, k1 from cn

⬭⤫ = 1/3 RC: Sl3 to cn, hold at back, k1, k3 from cn

⤬⬭ = 1/3 LC: Sl1 to cn, hold at front, k3, k1 from cn

⬭⤫ = 1/3 LPC: Sl3 to cn, hold at back, k1, p3 from cn

⤬⬭ = 1/3 RPC: Sl1 to cn, hold at front, p3, k1 from cn

Notre Dame Chart 2

Notre Dame Chart 4 (see p. 37 for rest of chart)

Notre Dame Chart 3 (see p. 36 for rest of chart)

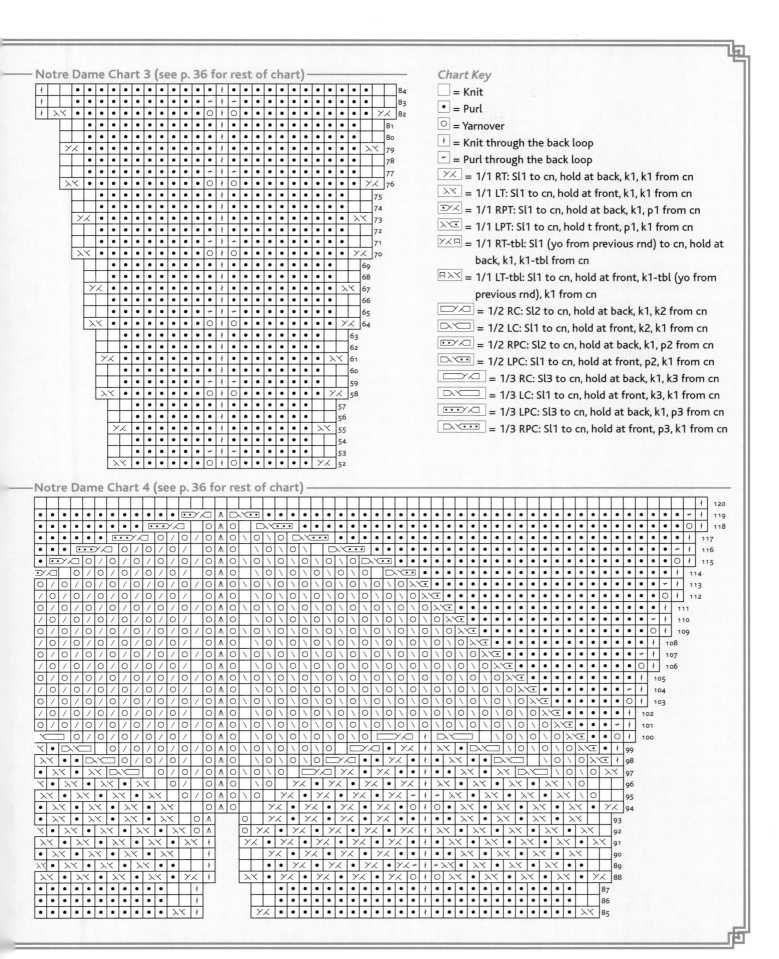

Chart Key

☐ = Knit

• = Purl

O = Yarnover

⊥ = Knit through the back loop

⟂ = Purl through the back loop

= 1/1 RT: Sl1 to cn, hold at back, k1, k1 from cn

= 1/1 LT: Sl1 to cn, hold at front, k1, k1 from cn

= 1/1 RPT: Sl1 to cn, hold at back, k1, p1 from cn

= 1/1 LPT: Sl1 to cn, hold t front, p1, k1 from cn

= 1/1 RT-tbl: Sl1 (yo from previous rnd) to cn, hold at back, k1, k1-tbl from cn

= 1/1 LT-tbl: Sl1 to cn, hold at front, k1-tbl (yo from previous rnd), k1 from cn

= 1/2 RC: Sl2 to cn, hold at back, k1, k2 from cn

= 1/2 LC: Sl1 to cn, hold at front, k2, k1 from cn

= 1/2 RPC: Sl2 to cn, hold at back, k1, p2 from cn

= 1/2 LPC: Sl1 to cn, hold at front, p2, k1 from cn

= 1/3 RC: Sl3 to cn, hold at back, k1, k3 from cn

= 1/3 LC: Sl1 to cn, hold at front, k3, k1 from cn

= 1/3 LPC: Sl3 to cn, hold at back, k1, p3 from cn

= 1/3 RPC: Sl1 to cn, hold at front, p3, k1 from cn

Notre Dame Chart 4 (see p. 36 for rest of chart)

Running Up That Hill Shawl
by Enrico Castronovo/Les Tricoteurs Volants

It should come as no surprise that I am obsessed with knitting, and particularly with the history of knitting. In many of the knitting books that I collect (which actually take up almost as much space as my stash), I have learnt how knitting techniques, stitches, and patterns have travelled in time and space, from the Middle East to Scandinavia, from Spain to Estonia, from Bavaria to Ireland, and from Europe to the New World. There is something in particular that fills me with tenderness in these books' images, that is knit samplers: these oblong rectangles in which anonymous knitters have got different stitches listed and classified, used to keep track of the traditional skills of a whole family or a whole village. These knitted pieces, often punched by moths, were the anchor point of a living community, almost like national flags.

One of the things that made me want to make my life in Paris is that you can meet History around every corner, in the hot touristic spots as well as in lesser-known neighborhoods. Just as for knitting, I am passionate about the history of Paris, the history of people who came from all over the world with their baggage and their own history to mold the city's face into its current shape, like a sampler of different stitches and textures that blend seamlessly in this shape that I love, rich from the diversities that make it up.

I have designed **Running Up That Hill** as a mini sampler, as my own little history of knitting: at the same time as the shawl's body is made in garter stitch, the border is formed by four different patterns running side by side, finding the way to shape a corner, and eventually changing direction altogether.

SIZE
One size

MATERIALS
Yarn by Simone MSW Fingering (100% Superwash Merino; 438 yd/400 m per 100 g skein); color: Rose des Bois; 2 skeins or approximately 720 m of fingering yarn
US5/3.75 mm needles for working flat (or size needed to achieve gauge)—single points or circular needle, as preferred
Cable needle, tapestry needle, stitch markers

GAUGE
20 sts x 40 rows = 4 inches/10 cm in Garter stitch, after blocking

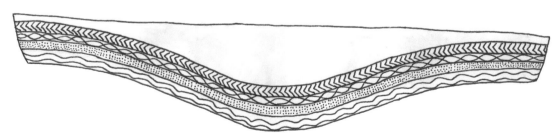

Finished Measurements
Wingspan: 77 inches/196 cm
Depth: 15¾ inches/40 cm

Yarn by Simone
Bourgogne, France
yarnbysimone.com
@yarnbysimone

SET-UP ROWS

CO 55 sts.

Row 1 (RS): Knit all sts.

Row 2 (WS): Knit to 3 last sts, sl3 wyif.

Repeat Rows 1–2 once more.

Repeat Row 1 once more.

Row 6 (WS): Kfb, k1, pl m, knit to last 3 sts, sl3 wyif—56 sts.

MAIN SECTION

Row 1 (RS): Work chart to m, sl m, ssk, knit to last st, kfb.

Row 2 (WS): Kfb, knit to m, sl m, work chart to end—1 st inc'd.

Repeat Rows 1–2, working the entire chart sixteen times for 256 rows—184 sts.

SHORT ROWS SECTION

Row 1 (RS): Work chart to st 38, wrap the next st, turn work.

Rows 2, 4 and 6 (WS): Work chart to end.

Row 3: Work chart to st 26, wrap the next st, turn work.

Row 5: Work chart to st 16, wrap the next st, turn work.

Row 7: Work to 1 st before the m according to the next row of the chart for every section, remove m, ssk, pl m—1 st dec'd.

Row 8: Sl1 wyif, work chart to end.

Work Rows 1–8 seven more times—176 sts. Remove marker.

KNIT-ON BORDER

Row 1 (RS): Work 52 sts according to the chart, k2tog-tbl (last st of the border and 1 st of the body of the shawl)—1 st dec'd.

Row 2 (WS): Sl1 wyif, work chart to end.

Repeat Rows 1–2, working the entire chart fifteen times for 240 rows from the beginning of the knit-on border—56 sts.

Next Row (RS): K52, k2tog-tbl—1 st dec'd.

Next Row (WS): Sl1 wyif, knit to 3 last sts, sl3 wyif.

Repeat last two rows once more.

Repeat RS row once more.

Bind off 53 remaining sts on the WS.

Finishing

Soak your shawl for about twenty minutes in slightly tepid water with mild soap, then squeeze gently and roll it in a clean towel to remove excess water. Lay flat on appropriate surface and block your shawl. Let dry, unpin, weave in ends, and wear proudly.

Running Up That Hill Pattern

Row 1 (RS): 1/2 LC, k1, (k1-tbl, k2) twice, k1-tbl, k4, k1b, k1, k1b, yo, ssk, yo, s2kpo, yo, k2tog, yo, k1b, k1, k1b, p2, k2-tbl, p2, k1-tbl, p2, k1b, k1, k1b, p2, k6, p2, k1b, k1, k1b.

Row 2 (WS): K5, p6, k7, p1-tbl, k2, p2-tbl, k5, p7, k7, (sl1 wyif, k2) twice, sl1 wyif, k1, sl3 wyif.

Row 3: K4, (1/1 LPT, k1) twice, 1/1 LPT, k3, (k1b, k1) twice, yo, ssk, k1, k2tog, yo, (k1, k1b) twice, p2, 2/1 LPT, 1/1 RPT, p2, k1b, k1, k1b, p2, 1/2 RC, 1/2 LC, p2, k1b, k1, k1b.

Row 4: K5, p6, k8, p3-tbl, k6, p7, k6, (sl1 wyif, k2) three times, sl3 wyif.

Row 5: 1/2 LC, k2, (1/1 LPT, k) twice, 1/1 LPT, k2, k1b, k1, k1b, yo, ssk, yo, s2kpo, yo, k2tog, yo, k1b, k1, k1b, p3, 2/1 LPT, p3, k1b, k1, k1b, p2, k6, p2, k1b, k1, k1b.

Row 6: K5, p6, k8, p3-tbl, k6, p7, k5, (sl1 wyif, k2) twice, sl1 wyif, k3, sl3 wyif.

Row 7: K6, (1/1 LPT, k1) three times, (k1b, k1) twice, yo, ssk, k1, k2tog, yo, (k1, k1b) twice, p2, 1/1 RPT, 2/1 LPT, p2, k1b, k1, k1b, p2, 1/2 RC, 1/2 LC, p2, k1b, k1, k1b.

Row 8: K5, p6, k7, p2-tbl, k2, p1-tbl, k5, p7, k4, (sl1 wyif, k2) twice, sl1 wyif, k4, sl3 wyif.

Row 9: 1/2 LC, k4, (k1-tbl, k2) twice, k1-tbl, (k1, k1b) twice, yo, ssk, yo, s2kpo, yo, k2tog, yo, k1b, k1, k1b, p2, k1-tbl, p2, k2-tbl, p2, k1b, k1, k1b, p2, k6, p2, k1b, k1, k1b.

Row 10: As Row 8.

Row 11: K6, (1/1 RPT, k1) three times, (k1b, k1) twice, yo, ssk, k1, k2tog, yo, (k1, k1b) twice, p2, 1/1 LPT, 2/1 RPT, p2, k1b, k1, k1b, p2, 1/2 RC, 1/2 LC, p2, k1b, k1, k1b.

Row 12: As Row 6.

Row 13: 1/2 LC, k2, (1/1 RPT, k1) twice, 1/1 RPT, k2, k1b, k1, k1b, yo, ssk, yo, s2kpo, yo, k2tog, yo, k1b, k1, k1b, p3, 2/1 RPT, p3, k1b, k1, k1b, p2, k6, p2, k1b, k1, k1b.

Row 14: As Row 4.

Row 15: K4, (1/1 RPT, k1) twice, 1/1 RPT, k3, (k1b, k1) twice, yo, ssk, k1, k2tog, yo, (k1, k1b) twice, p2, 2/1 RPT, 1/1 LPT, p2, k1b, k1, k1b, p2, 1/2 RC, 1/2 LC, p2, k1b, k1, k1b.

Row 16: As Row 2.

Running Up That Hill Chart

Chart Key

☐ = RS: Knit; WS: Purl	• = RS: Purl; WS: Knit	O = Yarnover	ƚ = Knit through the back loop	⋔ = Knit one below
\ = Ssk	/ = K2tog	⋀ = S2kpo	V = WS: Slip wyif	

⟋⟍ = 1/2 RC: Sl 2 to cn, hold at back, k1, k2 from cn

⟍⟋ = 1/2 LC: Sl 1 to cn, hold at front, k2, k1 from cn

⟋⟍ = 1/1 RPT: Sl 1 to cn, hold at back, k1-tbl, p1 from cn

⟍⟋ = 1/1 LPT: Sl 1 to cn, hold at front, p1, k1-tbl from cn

⟋⟍ = 2/1 RPT: Sl 1 to cn, hold at back, k2-tbl, p1 from cn

⟍⟋ = 2/1 LPT: Sl 2 to cn, hold at front, p1, k2-tbl from cn

Enrico loves Paris

What has your knitwear design journey been like?

When I started to knit, a bit more than 10 years ago, I made an ugly black mohair scarf. Then, my second project was a cardigan that I designed myself. That's what knitting has always meant to me: making things that I want to wear, in the colour, shape, and fabric that make my garment unique. A dozen projects and a billion stitches later, my knitting and non-knitting friends told me that I should share my designs just because they were beautiful and interesting. So I started to publish them on Ravelry, and I was very happy with the success they've met. One of my patterns has been Hot Right Now for 48 hours! And even today, the fact that a knitter on the other side of the planet is knitting a garment designed by me just makes me cheer!

Tell us a Paris story...

I've found myself face to face with **Louis Garrel** three times. And I love Louis Garrel. Who is, by the way, the most Parisian actor ever.

What is your favorite place in Paris?

There is a place in the heart of Paris, at the very centre of the city on the **Île de la Cité**, named **Place Dauphine**, and it's one of my favorite spots in Paris (and in the world, probably). One of the three sides of this small triangle is the **Palais de Justice** with its surrealistic snow-white staircase guarded by two marble lions. Little peaceful *terrasses* and art galleries are aligned on the two other sides, and the centre of the place is a solid ground with chestnut trees and benches. When I walk through Paris, and I walk a lot, I always try to pass by and pause for knitting or reading, overwhelmed by the magic of this little place, that André Breton called "the sex of Paris" due to its triangular shape.

Top Ten Books

1. Gérard de Nerval—*Aurélia* 2. Théophile Gautier—*Mademoiselle de Maupin* 3. Christopher Isherwood—*Goodbye to Berlin* 4. Philippe Le Guillou—*Les sept noms du peintre* 5. Jean Cocteau—*Les enfants terribles* 6. Antonin Artaud—*Héliogabale* 7. Jean Genet—*Querelle de Brest* 8. Eduardo Mendoza—*Sin noticias de Gurb* 9. H. P. Lovecraft—*Weird Tales* 10. Anne Rice—*Armand*

Top Ten Albums

1. Siouxsie & The Banshees—*A Kiss in the Dreamhouse* 2. Depeche Mode—*Music for the masses* 3. Joy Division—*Unknown Pleasures* 4. Kirlian Camera—*Pictures from Eternity* 5. The Cure—*Kiss me, kiss me, kiss me* 6. Bauhaus—*In the Flat Field* 7. The Smiths—*The Queen is Dead* 8. Cranes—*La Tragédie d'Oreste et Electre* 9. The Jesus & Mary Chain—*Psychocandy* 10. Curve—*Doppelgänger*

Top Ten TV Series

Twin Peaks. Because David Lynch is God, and Kyle MacLachlan is his prophet.

Torchwood. Because John Barrowman and Gareth David-Lloyd <3

Vikings. Because... well, Vikings!

True Blood. Because Blood is Life.

American Horror Story. Because the cast is just awesome.

Please like me. Because Josh Thomas looks like me when I was 20.

Family Guy. Because nothing makes me laugh more than that.

Downton Abbey. Because Lady Mary's outfits are to die for.

Misfits. Because Iwan Rheon is so sweet when out of Westeros.

Penny Dreadful. Because I would adore to have lunch with Eva Green.

Métro knitting: must-have or never ever?

Never ever. Because of people yelling "Look, a man who knits," or asking what I am knitting, or telling me "You don't have to worry, my auntie's neighbor is a knitter too, and he's even not gay," or "Oh... it reminds me of my father-in-law's cousin, he used to knit a lot when he was in the hospital," well, they just make me sick.

Favorite neighborhood?

Mine! I have lived in the district between the **Gare de l'Est** and the **Grands Boulevards** for 11 years, and five years ago I opened my shop **Les Tricoteurs Volants** in the same neighborhood. Far from the mainstream tourist spots, it's a living and friendly area, with bars and cafés, gastronomic groceries, design stores, and people from all over the world. The **Canal Saint-Martin** in the 10° is just five minutes away, and you can reach every point of the **Rive Droite** just walking on charming little streets.

Picker or thrower?

English-style picker, ma'am.

Project monogamy or cast on all the things?

I'm the most faithful person in the world when I'm in a relationship. But if it comes to knitting, with all the yarn to test and the beautiful designs to make, monogamy is just a surrealistic utopia. My average of WIPs is ... no, you don't want to know.

10° Arr: Les Tricoteurs Volants

Les Tricoteurs Volants
22, rue de la Fidélité, 10° Arr. • Tél: +33 1 47 70 52 57
Website: lestricoteursvolants.com • Instagram: @lestricoteursvolants

With a pink storefront and purple awning (owner Enrico's favorite color), Les Tricoteurs Volants is hard to miss. Once inside you will find ribbon, thread, buttons, the largest selection of knitting needles in Paris, an excellent selection of knitting books (including many School House Press titles), and lots and lots of lovely yarn from the likes of BC Garn, Borgo de' Pazzi, Rosy Green Wool, and more, plus some handspun by a Parisian friend. They offer a variety of classes for beginners and more advanced knitters and crocheters. When Enrico was deciding whether or not to open Les Tricoteurs Volants, he went to a nearby church to pray, where he looked up and saw the Spinning Madonna. Decision made!

*Right next door is the **Hôtel Grand Amour**. While we don't know anything about staying there, we can vouch for the lovely bistro on the ground floor with a delicious all-day menu plus outdoor seating in an Instagram-worthy inner courtyard.*

18° Arr: Les Petits Points Parisiens

Les Petits Points Parisiens
24, rue Véron, 18° Arr. • Tél: +33 1 72 34 77 37
Website: lespetitspointsparisiens.com •
Instagram: @lespetitspointsparisiens

After you make it to the top of Montmartre, reward yourself by walking downhill to this lovely little yarn shop (find a Brassaï-worthy *escalier*, if you can, to descend to rue Véron). Owner and dyer Anne is down-to-earth and lovely, and she has a great eye for color. In addition to her own line, Les Petits Points Parisiens stocks yarns from Fonty, Toft, The Uncommon Thread, and more, plus they carry fabric, sewing thread, and patterns. When you make a purchase, Anne will spritz a little Diptyque *parfum* in the bag—our yarn still has a lovely yet slight *eau de* what-we-have-come-to-consider-Montmartre. The shop offers classes and hosts a Knit Night every Thursday.

*Worked up an appetite with all those steps? Since we visited Montmartre right after our petit dejeuner, we can't give you a personal report, but we have heard great things about **Compagnie Generale de Biscuiterie**, **La Mascotte**, and **Café des Deux Moulins**.*

Tour Eiffel Shawl
by Julie Dubreux/Julie Knits In Paris

Towering dramatically over Paris since 1889, the Eiffel Tower has become the glittering symbol of the City of Light. Originally illuminated by hundreds of gas lamps, the tower now puts on a 20,000-bulb golden light show every night with five minutes of magical flickering at the top of every hour.

What is amazing about the tower is that everything is integral to the structure. The only non-essential elements are the four decorative grill-work arches on the first level.

Tour Eiffel is a half-pi shawl featuring the tower's four legs and cables re-creating the cast iron work that decorates the arches of La Grande Dame de Fer.

I chose an ombré yarn for this design because, funnily enough, the Eiffel Tower is painted in 3 different hues, from a darker bottom part to a lighter top part! Indeed, the precisely-engineered iron beams are much closer to one another towards the top, so it would look much darker than the bottom if it was painted the same colour. The gradient is the only way to create the illusion that the colour of the tower is uniform!

SIZE
One size

MATERIALS
La Fée Fil Merino Nylon Ombré Fingering (75% Merino, 25% Nylon; 1395 yd/1275 m per 10.5 oz/300 g skein); color: Paris la nuit; 1 skein or approximately 1250 m fingering yarn

US4/3.5 mm circular needle, 40-inch/100 cm (or size needed to achieve gauge)—long needle used to accommodate the large number of stitches

Stitch markers, cable needle, tapestry needle

GAUGE
20 sts x 28 rows = 4 inches/10 cm in Garter stitch, after blocking

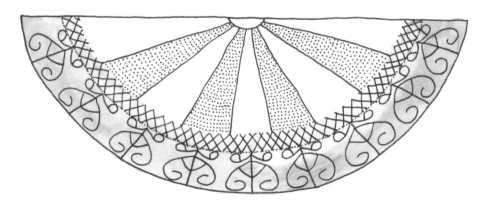

Finished Measurements
Wingspan: 67 inches/170 cm
Depth: 32 inches/80 cm

La Fée Fil
Oise, France
lafeefil.fr
@lafeefil

SECTION 1 : TOWER LEGS

CO 2 sts.

Set-up Row 1 (RS): K2.

Set-up Row 2 (WS): P2.

Repeat the last 2 rows once more.

Set-up Row 5: K2, pick up and knit 4 sts along side edge, pick up and knit 2 sts along cast-on edge—8 sts.

Set-up Row 6: Purl to end.

Set-up Row 7: K2, (m1-L, k1) to last 2 sts, m1-L, k2—13 sts.

Set-up Row 8: P2, knit to last 2 sts, p2.

Set-up Row 9: K2, (yo, k1) to last 2 sts, yo, k2—23 sts.

Set-up Row 10: P2, knit to last 2 sts, p2.

Set-up Row 11: K2, m1-L, knit to last 2 sts, m1-L, k2—2 sts inc'd.

Set-up Row 12: P2, knit to last 2 sts, p2.

Work last 2 rows once more—27 sts.

Set-up Row 15: K2, m1-L, (k2tog, yo) to last 3 sts, k1, m1-L, k2—29 sts.

Set-up Row 16: P2, knit to last 2 sts, p2.

Set-up Row 17: K3, (pl m, sl2, k1) 8 times, k2.

Set-up Row 18: P2, knit to 2 sts before m, p2, sl m) 8 times, knit to last 2 sts, p2.

Row 1 (RS): K2, m1-L, (knit to m, m1-L, sl m, sl2 sts, m1-L) eight times, knit to last 2 sts, m1-L, k2—18 sts inc'd.

Row 2 and all other WS rows (WS): P2, knit to 2 sts before m, p2, sl m) eight times, knit to last 2 sts, p2.

Row 3 (RS): (Knit to m, sl m, sl2 sts) eight times, knit to end.

Row 5 (RS): *Knit to m, sl m, sl2 sts, (k2tog, yo) to 1 st before m, k1, sl m, sl2 sts.* Repeat from * to * three more times, knit to end.

Row 7 (RS): (Knit to m, sl m, sl2 sts) eight times, knit to end.

Work Rows 1–8 for 19 more times—389 sts.

SECTION 2: CAST-IRON BORDER

Row 1 (RS): K2, m1-F, p2, m1-F, (p12, m1-F) 3 times, p2, m1-F, p1, m1-F, *slm, k2, m1-F, p1, (p10, m1-F) 4 times.* Repeat from * to * seven more times, k2—436 sts.

Row 2 (WS): P2, k6, (k4, p4, k4) to last 8 sts slipping ms as you go, k6, p2.

Work Tour Eiffel Chart 1 for 14 rows (see p. 47).

Row 3 (RS): K2, purl to last 2 sts, k2, removing ms as you go.

Row 4 (WS): P2, (k48, pl m) eight times, k48, p2.

Work Tour Eiffel Chart 2 for 15 rows (see p. 47).

Row 5 (RS): K2, purl to last 2 sts, k2.

Row 6 (WS): *K2, k2tog-tbl, sl3 back onto left hand needle.* Repeat from * to * until there 3 sts remain. Break yarn and pull thread through last 3 sts.

Finishing

Weave in ends and block to finished measurements.

Tour Eiffel Chart 1

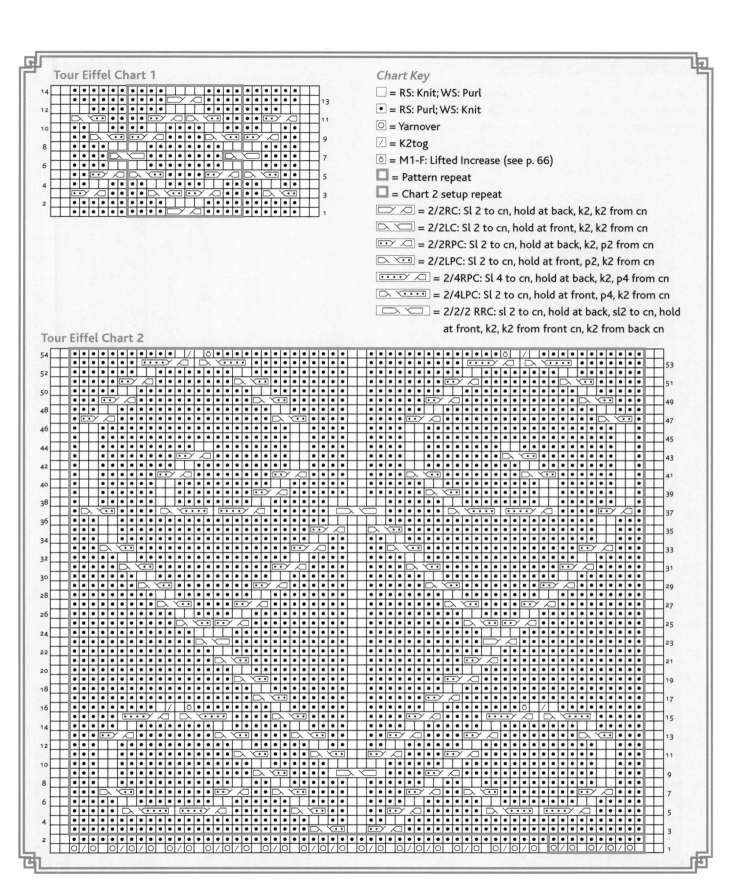

What has your knitwear design journey been like?

I'm really more of a collector of knitwear designs, and my journey started where so many knitting ships have been launched—the hallowed shores of Ravelry. I don't remember learning how to knit or read, but I remember exactly where I was when I got my Beta invitation to Ravelry.

Tell us a Paris story...

The summer before my sophomore year in college, I worked in Paris as a nanny to four French kids who didn't speak any English. Which worked out great because I didn't speak any French. I mimed my way through the summer while we toured Normandy in a maroon Chrysler minivan, stuffing chocolate bars in hollowed-out baguettes for an instant *pan au chocolat* and discovering the buttery joy of raw milk Camembert de Normandie. I also got a priceless education in French manners, customs, history, and culture from the front lines.

Métro knitting: must-have or never ever?

Must-have. Knitting optimism dictates there might be a chance to put a couple more rows on your project, so I've always got it at the ready. Usually stockinette, in the round if I'm really planning ahead. And the number of knitters you meet is remarkable!

Favorite station?

Perverse as it may be, I love the **Montmartre** station because of all the stairs. Previously anonymous metro riders form a *peloton* climbing up endless spiral stairs until... VOILA! We emerge with a collective gasp for air. It's a Paris moment!

Picker or thrower?

Thrower, but I think my trademark "firm" knitting gauge might benefit from learning Continental.

Project monogamy or cast on all the things?

All the things, always. I regularly buy needles and yarn at the same time so I can cast on immediately. I've got a drawer full of circular

US6 needles that will attest to this habit. I bought yarn at every shop we visited in Paris and I think I must have cast on at least three projects while we were there.

Favorite places to knit in Paris?

Parisians are a lucky bunch, favored with beautiful parks and gardens outfitted with wonderful cafés that serve simple, delicious food (and carafes of wine!) Check out **Jardin du Luxembourg**, **Jardin des Tuileries**, **Jardin du Palais Royal**, and **Les Jardins du Trocadero** for amazing settings with spectacular views, and a chance to relax away from the hustle and bustle of Paris. Get a table with a view, take out your knitting, and you're set for a while. I'd recommend something you don't have to pay too close attention—save your complicated cable work for later—and enjoy La Vie en Rose!

13° Arr: La Bien Aimée

La Bien Aimée
89, avenue d'Italie, 13° Arr. • Tél : +33 1 43 40 08 19
Website: labienaimee.com • Instagram: @labienaimee

Just look for the bright yellow storefront, as you make your way down avenue d'Italie, and before you know it you will be enveloped by the smell of wet wool, since Aimée dyes her yarns here in the back of the shop. In addition to her own line, she carries Biches et Buches, Woolfolk, De Rerum Natura, and others, along with Fringe Field Bags, Merchant & Mills notions, various needles, enamel pins from Shellican, and books and magazines. The staff are multilingual, friendly, and helpful. You will find comfy spots to sit and knit in this bright white yet cozy space.

On your walk from La Bien Aimée to L'OisiveThé, don't miss the artesian well that still provides water to locals and passersby alike. Be sure to fill up your water bottle, just like they've been doing since 1863. Both shops have a little postcard map that points out the well along the route between the two.

13° Arr: L'OisiveThé

L'OisiveThé
8 bis, rue de la Butte aux Cailles, 13° Arr. • Tél : +33 1 53 80 31 33
Website: loisivethe.com • Instagram: @loisivethe

A few blocks away from La Bien Aimée is Aimée's original knitting shop and tea salon, which also serves the best cookie in Paris. In addition to being a charming café, they stock yarn from Titus, Wollmeise, Quince & Co., Magpie, and many more, plus books and patterns. There are toys and games to occupy children, a library of knitting books to consult, and windows on two sides for eyeing your color choices in daylight. They host a *salon de thé et tricot* for 22 lucky knitters every Wednesday evening. Visit their Ravelry group for details: *ravelry.com/groups/loisivethe-salon-de-the-et-tricot*

The salon has both indoor and outdoor seating and serves a wide selection of teas stored in the charming yellow canisters displayed on the back wall, as well as coffee, soda, beer, wine, and cider. They serve a variety of savory dishes and sweets, as well as a weekend brunch.

A Tower in Paris Pullover
by Marion Crivelli

Although the movies make you think you can see the Eiffel Tower from any window in Paris, the reality is that, with most buildings limited to a height of seven stories, there are few places where you have a clear view of the tower. Why not create your very own Tower out of cables?

What was once controversial (300 writers, painters, sculptors, and architects—one for each meter of the tower's proposed height—formed a committee in 1887 to protest the design, which they called a barbaric blot of ink upon the beauty of Paris) is now a beloved landmark visited by seven million people per year. Gustave Eiffel and company may have only expected the tower to stand for

20 years, but it is clearly a monument for the ages.

A Tower in Paris is knitted from the top down seamlessly. You start with a ribbed neckline in two parts, then join for working in the round by increasing the sleeves, then make raglan increases for the sleeves and body, then separate the body and sleeves, and finally work the body in the round to the end. There are cables (to represent the Eiffel Tower) and reverse stockinette on the front. The back is knitted in reverse stockinette. The hem is worked with cable and I-cord. The sleeves are knit last, in the round, in stockinette stitch, and finished as for the body.

SIZES

XS (S, M, L, 1X, 2X, 3X) to fit bust sizes 28 (32, 36, 40, 44, 48, 52) inches/71 (81, 91, 101, 111, 122, 132) cm, shown in size S with 2 inches/5 cm of ease

MATERIALS

La Fée Fil Single Mérinos Fingering (100% Merino; 394 yd/360 m per 3½ oz/100 g skein); color: Ernest; 3.5 (3.5, 4, 4.5, 5, 5.5, 6) skeins or approximately 1312 (1312, 1530, 1640, 1860, 2080, 2300) yd/1200 (1200, 1400, 1500, 1700, 1900, 2100) m of fingering yarn

US4/3.5 mm circular needle, 47-inch/120 cm + set of DPNs (or size needed to achieve gauge)

US2½/3.0 mm circular needle, 47-inch/120 cm + set of DPNs (or approximately 0.5 mm smaller than gauge needle)

Stitch markers, cable needle, tapestry needle

GAUGE

25 sts x 32 rnds = 4 inches/10 cm in reverse Stockinette stitch with larger needle, after blocking

Finished Measurements
Bust circumference: 31¼ (34¼, 40, 42½, 48¼, 50¾, 54½) inches/79.25 (87.25, 101.5, 108, 122.5, 128.75, 138.5) cm
Length from underarm to hem: 17¼ inches/44 cm for all sizes
Yoke depth: 7¾ (8½, 9, 9½, 9¾, 10½, 11) inches/20 (22, 23, 24, 25, 27, 28) cm.
Upper sleeve circumference: 10¼ (11½, 12¼, 13¼, 15, 16, 17) inches/25.5 (28.75, 30.5, 32.75, 37.5, 40, 42.5) cm
Sleeve length from armhole to cuff: 17 inches/43 cm for all sizes

La Fée Fil
Oise, France
lafeefil.fr
@lafeefil

COLLAR

Work with smaller circular needle.

Back: CO 90 (93, 96, 96, 99, 102, 102) sts. Do not join. Work in 2/1 Twisted Rib (see p. 66) until your piece measures 1½ inches/4 cm from CO edge. Cut yarn and place on holder.

Front: CO 69 (72, 75, 75, 78, 81, 81) sts. Do not join. Work in 2/1 Twisted Rib until your piece measures 1½ inches/4 cm from CO edge.

YOKE

Switch to larger circular needle.

You will now join the two pieces for working in the rnd. *Note: All sizes except S and XL make one inc on the middle of front m1-Rp. Sizes S and XL only make one dec p2tog on the middle of back.*

RS: Purl all sts of front to 5 sts before end, sl these 5 sts to cable needle, hold in font, *p2tog the first st of cn and the first st of back; rep from * four more times, pl m1, k8, pl m2, purl to 13 sts before end of back collar, pl m3, k8, pl mBOR, sl the last 5 sts to cn, hold in back, *p2tog the first st of front and the first st of cn; rep from * four more times—150 (154, 162, 162, 166, 174, 174) sts: 70 (72, 76, 76, 78, 82, 82) sts for front, 64 (66, 70, 70, 72, 76, 76) sts for back and 8 sts for each sleeve. Switch to larger needle.

Shape shoulder with short rows

Note: To shape the neck, you will work back and forth around the left shoulder, then back and forth around the right shoulder.

Shape left shoulder

Short Row 1 (RS): Purl to m1, sl m1, m1-R, knit to m2, m1-L, sl m2, k4, W&T.
Short Row 2 (WS): Purl to m2, sl m2, m1-Rp, purl to m1, m1-Lp, sl m1, k4, W&T.
Short Row 3 (RS): Purl to m1, sl m1, m1-R, knit to m2, m1-Lp, sl m2, purl to last wrapped st, pick up wrap and purl it together with st, W&T.
Short Row 4 (WS): Knit to m2, sl m2, m1-Rp, purl to m1, m1-Lp, sl m1, knit to last wrapped st, pick up wrap and knit it together with st, W&T.
Rep Short Rows 3&4 three more times—70 (72, 76, 76, 78, 82, 82) sts for front, 64 (66, 70, 70, 72, 76, 76) sts for left sleeve.

Shape right shoulder

Short Row 1 (RS): Purl to m1, sl m1, knit to

m2, sl m2, purl to m3 (pick up wrap and purl it together with st when you come to it), sl m3, m1-R, knit to mBOR, m1-L, sl mBOR, p4, W&T.
Short Row 2 (WS): Knit to mBOR, sl mBOR, m1-Rp, purl to m3, m1-Lp, sl m3, k4, W&T.
Short Row 3 (RS): Purl to m3, sl m3, m1-R, knit to mBOR, m1-L, sl mBOR, purl to last wrapped st, pick up wrap and purl it together with st, W&T.
Short Row 4 (WS): Knit to mBOR, sl mBOR, m1-Rp, purl to m3, m1-Lp, sl m3, knit to last wrapped st, pick up wrap and knit it together with st, W&T.
Rep Short Rows 3&4 three more times—70 (72, 76, 76, 78, 82, 82) sts for front, 64 (66, 70, 70, 72, 76, 76) sts for back and 28 sts for each sleeve.
Next Row (RS): Purl to m3, sl m3, knit to mBOR.

Set up cable and raglan increase

Set up Round: Sl mBOR (new m4), p18 (19, 21, 21, 22, 24, 24), pl mC, k16, p2, k16, pl mC, purl to m1 (new mBOR).

Increase back and sleeves

Rnd 1: Sl mBOR, k1, m1-R, knit to 1 st before m2, m1-L, k1, sl m2, p1, m1-Rp, purl to 1 st before m3, m1-Lp, p1, sl m3, k1, m1-R, knit to 1 st before m4, m1-L, k1, sl m4, purl to mC, sl mC, work Rnd 1 of Cable A, p2, work Rnd 1 of Cable A, sl mC, purl to end—6 sts inc'd.
Rnd 2: Sl mBOR, knit to m2, sl m2, purl to m3, sl m3, knit to m4, sl m4, purl to mC, sl mC, work rnd 2 of Cable A, p2, work rnd 2 of Cable A, sl mC, purl to end—70 (72, 76, 76, 78, 82, 82) sts for front, 66 (68, 72, 72, 74, 78, 78) sts for back and 30 sts for each sleeve.
Rnd 3: Sl mBOR, k1, m1-R, knit to 1 st before m2, m1-L, k1, sl m2, p1, m1-Rp, purl to 1 st before m3, m1-Lp, p1, sl m3, k1, m1-R, knit to 1 st before m4, m1-L, k1, sl m4, purl to mC, sl mC, work the next rnd of Cable A, p2, work the next rnd of Cable A, sl mC, purl to end—6 sts inc'd.
Rnd 4: Sl mBOR, knit to m2, sl m2, purl to m3, sl m3, knit to m4, sl m4, purl to mC, sl mC, work the next rnd of Cable A, p2, work the next rnd of Cable A, sl mC, purl to end—70 (72, 76, 76, 78, 82, 82) sts for front, 68 (70, 74, 74, 76, 80, 80) sts for back and 32 sts for each sleeve.

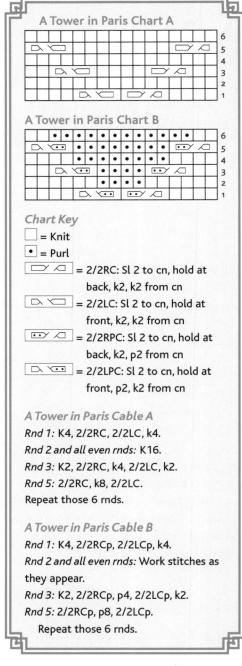

Rep Rnds 3&4 once more—70 (72, 76, 76, 78, 82, 82) sts for front and for back, 34 sts for each sleeve.

Increase back, front and sleeve

Rnd 5: Sl mBOR, k1, m1-R, knit to 1 st before m2, m1-L, k1, sl m2, p1, m1-Rp, purl to 1 st before m3, m1-Lp, p1, sl m3, k1, m1-R, knit to 1 st before m4, m1-L, k1, sl m4, p1, m1-Rp, purl to mC, sl mC, work the next rnd of Cable A, p2, work the next rnd of Cable A, sl mC, purl to 1 st before end, m1-Lp, p1—8 sts inc'd.
Rnd 6: Sl mBOR, knit to m2, sl m2, purl to m3, sl m3, knit to m4, sl m4, purl to mC, sl

mC, work the next rnd of Cable A, p2, work the next rnd of Cable A, sl mC, purl to end —72 (74, 78, 78, 80, 84, 84) sts for front and for back, 36 sts for each sleeve.

Rep Rounds 5&6 for 12 (14, 14, 14, 14, 14) times total—96 (102, 106, 106, 108, 112, 112) sts for back and for front, 60 (64, 64, 64, 64, 64, 64) sts for each sleeve.

For Size XS, if necessary, work as explained without increasing until your body measures about 7¾ inches/20 cm from CO row ending with Rnd 4 of Cable A (measuring along front raglan) and skip to Dividing Body and Sleeves.

Sizes — (S, M, L, 1X, 2X, 3X) only

Rnd 7: Sl mBOR, k1, m1-R, knit to 1 st before m2, m1-L, k1, sl m2, p1, m1-Rp, purl to 1 st before m3, m1-Lp, p1, sl m3, k1, m1-R, knit to 1 st before m4, m1-L, k1, sl m4, p1, m1-Rp, purl to mC, sl mC, work the next rnd of Cable A, pfb, pfb, work the next rnd of Cable A, sl mC, purl to 1 st before end, m1-Lp, p1—10 sts inc'd.

Rnd 8: Sl mBOR, knit to m2, sl m2, purl to m3, sl m3, knit to m4, sl m4, purl to mC, sl mC, work the next rnd of Cable A, p4, work the next rnd of Cable A, sl mC, purl to end— XS (106, 110, 110, 112, 116, 116) sts for front, XS (104, 108, 108, 110, 114, 114) sts for back and 66 sts for each sleeve.

Rnd 9: Sl mBOR, k1, m1-R, knit to 1 st before m2, m1-L, k1, sl m2, p1, m1-Rp, purl to 1 st before m3, m1-Lp, p1, sl m3, k1, m1-R, knit to 1 st before m4, m1-L, k1, sl m4, p1, m1-Rp, purl to mC, sl mC, work the next rnd of Cable A, p4, work the next rnd of Cable A, sl mC, purl to 1 st before end, m1-Lp, p1—8 sts inc'd.

Rnd 10: Sl mBOR, knit to m2, sl m2, purl to m3, sl m3, knit to m4, sl m4, purl to mC, sl mC, work the next rnd of Cable A, p4, work the next rnd of Cable A, sl mC, purl to end— XS (108, 112, 112, 114, 118, 118) sts for front, XS (106, 110, 110, 112, 116, 116) sts for back and 68 sts for each sleeve.

Size S, if necessary, work as explained without increasing until Body measures about 8½ inches/20 cm from CO row ending with Rnd 4 of Cable A (measuring along front raglan) and skip to Dividing Body and Sleeves.

Sizes — (—, M, L, 1X, 2X, 3X) only

Rep Rounds 9&10 for XS (S, 2, 5, 10, 13, 16) more times— XS (S, 116, 122, 134, 144, 150) sts for front, XS (S, 114, 120, 132, 142, 148)

sts for back and XS (S, 72, 78, 88, 94, 100) sts for each sleeve.

Increase body only

Rnd 11: Sl mBOR, knit to m2, sl m2, p1, m1-Rp, purl to 1 st before m3, m1-Lp, p1, sl m3, knit to m4, sl m4, p1, m1-Rp, purl to mC, sl mC, work the next rnd of Cable A, p4, work the next rnd of Cable A, sl mC, purl to 1 st before end, m1-Lp, p1—4 sts inc'd.

Rnd 12: Sl mBOR, knit to m2, sl m2, purl to m3, sl m3, knit to m4, sl m4, purl to mC, sl mC, work the next rnd of Cable A, p4, work the next rnd of Cable A, sl mC, purl to end.

Rep Rnds 11&12 for XS (S, 4, 5, 7, 6, 9) more times—XS (S, 126, 134, 150, 158, 170) sts for front, XS (S, 124, 132, 148, 156, 168) sts for back and XS (S, 72, 78, 88, 94, 100) sts for each sleeve.

If necessary, work as explained without increasing until Body measures about XS (S, 9, 9½, 9¾, 10½, 11) inches/XS (S, 23, 24, 25, 27, 28) cm from CO row ending with Rnd 4 of Cable A (measuring along front raglan) and skip to Dividing Body and Sleeves.

You must separate body and sleeves by knitting Rnd 5 of Cable A. If it isn't where you are in the pattern when you finish your

increases, continue to work as explained without increasing, ending with Rnd 4 of Cable A before Dividing Body and Sleeves.

DIVIDING BODY AND SLEEVES
Size XS only

Next Rnd: Sl mBOR (remove mBOR), CO 1 st, pl mBOR (remove m2), pl next 60 sts on hold, CO 1 st, purl to m3 (remove m3), CO 1 st, pl m (remove m4), pl next 60 sts on hold, CO 1 st, purl to mC, sl mC, work Rnd 5 of Cable A, pfb, pfb, work Rnd 5 of Cable A, sl mC, purl to mBOR.

Sizes — (S, M, L, 1X, 2X, 3X) only

Next Rnd: Remove mBOR, CO XS (1, 1, 1, 2, 2, 2) st(s), pl mBOR, pl the next XS (68, 72, 78, 88, 94, 100) sts on hold, (remove m2), CO XS (1, 1, 1, 2, 2, 2) st(s), purl to m3 (remove m3), CO XS (1, 1, 1, 2, 2, 2) st(s), pl m, pl the next XS (68, 72, 78, 88, 94, 100) sts on hold, (remove m4), CO XS (1, 1, 1, 2, 2, 2) st(s), purl to mC, sl mC, work Rnd 5 of Cable A, p4, work Rnd 5 of Cable A, sl mC, purl to mBOR.

All sizes

Note: You will remove the mC and place a new mC in the middle of the 4 purled sts

Next Rnd: Sl mBOR, purl to m, sl m, purl to

mC, sl mC (remove mC), work Rnd 6 of Cable A, p2, pl mC, p2, work Rnd 6 of Cable A, sl mC (remove mC), purl to end—198 (218, 254, 270, 306, 322, 346) sts for body; 100 (110, 128, 136, 154, 162, 174) sts for front, 98 (108, 126, 134, 152, 160, 172) sts for back and 60 (68, 72, 78, 88, 94, 100) sts on hold for each sleeve.

BODY

Set up Rnd: Sl mBOR, purl to m, sl m, purl to 24 sts before mC (middle of purled sts), pl mC (remove the next mC), work Rnd 1 of Cable A 3 times, pl mC, purl to end.

Rnd 1: Sl mBOR, purl to m, sl m, purl to mC, sl mC, work the next rnd of Cable A three times, sl mC, purl to end.

Rep Rnd 1 four more times (or until you have worked the 6 rnds of Cable A).

Rnd 2: Sl mBOR, purl to m, sl m, purl to mC, sl mC, work Rnd 1 of Cable A, Rnd 1 of Cable B, Rnd 1 of Cable A, sl mC, purl to end.

Rnd 3: Sl mBOR, purl to m, sl m, purl to mC, sl mC, work the next rnd of Cable A, the next rnd of Cable B, the next rnd of Cable A, sl mC, purl to end.

Rep Rnd 3 four more times (or until you have worked the 6 rnds of cables).

At the same time, when your piece measures 3 inches/8 cm from armhole, make body increases as follows:

Odd Rnd—Increase Body: Sl mBOR, p8, m1-Lp, purl to 8 sts before m, m1-Rp, p8, sl m, p8, m1-Lp, purl to mC, sl mC, work as explain to mC, sl mC, purl to 8 sts before end, m1-Rp, p8—4 sts inc'd.

Rep Increase Rnd every 10 (10, 10, 10, 12, 12, 14) rnds, 5 (8, 7, 7, 6, 6, 4) more times. 222 (254, 286, 302, 334, 350, 366) sts for the body.

Rnd 4: Sl mBOR, purl to m, sl m, purl to mC, sl mC, work Rnd 1 of Cable A, pl mC, p16, pl mC, work Rnd 1 of Cable A, sl mC, purl to end.

Rnd 5: Sl mBOR, purl to m, sl m, purl to mC, sl mC, work the next rnd of Cable A, sl mC, p16, sl mC, work the next rnd of Cable A, sl mC, purl to end.

Rep Rnd 5 ten more times (or until you have worked the 6 rnds of Cable A, two times in total).

Move cable

Note: Continue to increase for the body as explained above.

Rnd 6: Sl mBOR, purl to m, sl m, purl to 2 sts before mC, p2tog, sl mC, work Rnd 1 of Cable A, sl mC, p1, m1-Lp, purl to 1 st before mC, m1-Rp, p1, sl mC, work Rnd 1 of Cable A, sl mC, ssp, purl to end.

Rnd 7: Sl mBOR, purl to m, sl m, purl to mC, sl mC, work the next rnd of Cable A, sl mC, p18, sl mC, work the next rnd of Cable A, sl mC, purl to end.

Rep Rnd 7 ten more times (or until you have worked the 6 rnds of Cable A, two times in total).

Rnd 8: Sl mBOR, purl to m, sl m, purl to 2 sts before mC, p2tog, sl mC, work the Rnd 1 of Cable A, sl mC, p1, m1-Lp, purl to 1 st before mC, m1-Rp, p1, sl mC, work Rnd 1 of Cable A, sl mC, ssp, purl to end.

Rnd 9: Sl mBOR, purl to m, sl m, purl to mC, sl mC, work the next rnd of Cable A, sl mC, p20, sl mC, work the next rnd of Cable A, sl mC, purl to end.

Rep Rnd 9, ten more times (or until you have worked the 6 rnds of Cable A, two times in total).

Rnd 10: Sl mBOR, purl to m, sl m, purl to 6 sts before mC, pl mC (remove the 3 next mC), work Rnd 1 of Cable A four times, pl mC, purl to end.

Rnd 11: Sl mBOR, purl to m, sl m, purl to mC, sl mC, work the next rnd of Cable A four times, sl mC, purl to end.

Rep Rnd 11 sixteen more times (or until you have worked the 6 rnds of Cable A, three times in total).

Rnd 12: Sl mBOR, purl to m, sl m, purl to mC, sl mC, work Rnd 1 of Cable A, Rnd 1 of Cable B two times, Rnd 1 of Cable A, sl mC, purl to end.

Rnd 13: Sl mBOR, purl to m, sl m, purl to mC, sl mC, work the next rnd of Cable A, next rnd of Cable B two times, next rnd of Cable A, sl mC, purl to end.

Rep Rnd 13 four more times (or until you have worked the 6 rnds of cables).

Rnd 14: Sl mBOR, purl to m, sl m, purl to mC, sl mC, work Rnd 1 of Cable A, pl mC, p32, pl mC, work Rnd 1 of Cable A, sl mC, purl to end.

Rnd 15: Sl mBOR, purl to m, sl m, purl to mC, sl mC, work the next rnd of Cable A, sl mC, p32, sl mC, work the next rnd of Cable A, sl mC, purl to end.

Rep Rnd 15 four more times (or until you have worked the 6 rnds of Cable A).

Rnd 16: Sl mBOR, purl to m, sl m, purl to 2 sts before mC, p2tog, sl mC, work the next rnd of Cable A, sl mC, p1, m1-Lp, purl to 1 st before mC, m1-Rp, p1, sl mC, work the next rnd of Cable A, sl mC, ssp, purl to end.

Rnd 17: Sl mBOR, purl to m, sl m, purl to mC, sl mC, work the next rnd of Cable A, sl mC, purl to mC, sl mC, work the next rnd of Cable A, sl mC, purl to end.

Rep Rnd 17 four more times (or until you have worked the 6 rnds of Cable A).

Then *work Rnd 16 and repeat Rnd 17 five times in total; repeat from * 7 more times (or until you have 48 sts purled between the two cables)

If necessary, work as follows: Sl mBOR, purl to m, sl m, purl to mC, sl mC, work the next rnd of Cable A, sl mC, purl to mC, sl mC, work the next rnd of Cable A, sl mC, purl to end; until your body measures 15¾ inches/40 cm from armhole or 1½ inches/4 cm than less desired length ending with Rnd 6 of Cable A.

HEM

Next Rnd: Sl mBOR (remove mBOR), p1, m1-Lp, purl to m, sl m (remove m), p1, m1-Lp, purl to mC, sl mC (remove mC), pl mBOR, work Rnd 1 of Cable A to end - 14 (16, 18, 19, 21, 22, 23) cable repeats in total—224 (256, 288, 304, 336, 352, 368) sts for the body.

Next Rnd: Sl mBOR, work the next rnd of Cable A to end.

Rep this last rnd sixteen more times (or until you have worked the 6 rnds of Cable A three times in total).

Switch to smaller circular needle and work I-cord Bind-Off (see p. 66) until you have bound off all sts (3 sts remain on your right

needle). To finish you will graft the last three sts together with the first three sts, creating a seamless join to your I-cord.

SLEEVES

Place the sts on hold for one sleeve on larger circular needle or DPNs. Attach yarn and starting from middle of underarm, pick up and knit 2 (2, 2, 2, 3, 3, 3) sts, k60 (68, 72, 78, 88, 94, 100) sts for one sleeve, pick up and knit 2 (2, 2, 2, 3, 3, 3) sts, pl mBOR—64 (72, 76, 82, 94, 100, 106) sts.

Rnd 1: Sl mBOR, knit to end.

Rep Rnd 1, until your sleeve measure 2 inches/5 cm from armhole.

Decrease Round: Sl mBOR, k1, ssk, knit to 3 sts before end, k2tog, k1—62 (70, 74, 80, 92, 98, 104) sts on your needle.

Rep Decrease Rnd every 3 (2¼, 2¼, 2, 1¼, ¾, ¾) inch(es)/8 (6, 6, 5, 3, 2, 2) cm, 2 (5, 5, 6, 10, 12, 14) more times—58 (60, 64, 68, 72, 74, 76) sts on your needle.

Continue to work Rnd 1 until your sleeve measure 15¼ inches/39 cm from armhole or 1½ inches/4 cm then less desired length On the last rnd:

Size XS: K2tog, knit to end.

Size 2X: K2tog, knit to 2 sts before end, ssk.

You should have: 57 (60, 64, 68, 72, 72, 76) sts on your needle.

CUFF

Sizes XS (S) only

Rnd 1: Sl mBOR, *p3 (4), work Rnd 1 of Cable A; repeat from * 2 more times.

Rnd 2: Sl mBOR, *p3 (4), work the next Rnd of Cable A; repeat from * 2 more times.

Rep Rnd 2 until you have worked the 6 rnds of Cable A three times in total.

Size M only

Rnd 1: Sl mBOR, work Rnd 1 of Cable A four times.

Rnd 2: Sl mBOR, work the next Rnd of Cable A four times.

Repeat Rnd 2 until you have worked the 6 rnds of Cable A three times in total.

Sizes L (1X, 2X, 3X) only

Rnd 1: Sl mBOR, *p1 (2, 2, 3), work Rnd 1 of Cable A; repeat from * three more times.

Rnd 2: Sl mBOR, *p1 (2, 2, 3), work the next rnd of Cable A; repeat from * three more times.

Rep Rnd 2 until you have worked the 6 rnds

of Cable A three times in total.

All sizes

Switch to smaller circular needle and work I-cord Bind-Off until you have bound off all sts (3 sts remain on your right needle). To finish you will graft the last three sts together with the first three sts, creating a seamless join to your I-cord.

Finishing

For the collar, sew both ends together. Weave in all ends. Block to finished measurements.

Tuileries Pullover
by Julie Dubreux/Julie Knits In Paris

Tuileries is a comfortable and stylish sweater with an oversize collar you can snuggle into when you lounge on the famous green garden furniture in Jardin des Tuileries.

It is worked in the round from the top down and is completely seamless.

The twisted ribbing featured in the collar is echoed in the long fitted sleeves, which contrast with the cropped and boxy body in plain stockinette stitch.

When I designed this sweater, I remembered my student days in Paris when I would relax and read in les Tuileries or Jardin du Luxembourg.

Tuileries could be worn under a feminine leather jacket, just like the one Catherine Deneuve chose to wear when she was photographed by Jean-Loup Sieff in Jardin des Tuileries. A friend of mine was lucky enough to witness this iconic photoshoot happening, so we were all fascinated with the pictures when they were published, and to this day these images come to mind every time I stroll around Les Tuileries.

SIZE

XS (S, M, L, 1X, 2X, 3X) to fit bust sizes 28 (32, 36, 40, 44, 48, 52) inches/71 (81, 91, 101, 111, 122, 132) cm, shown in size S with 7 inches/17 cm of positive ease

MATERIALS

De Rerum Natura Ulysse (100% Merino; 202 yd/185 m per 1.76 oz/50 g skein); color: Goeland; 7 (7, 8, 9, 10, 11, 12) skeins or approximately 1200 (1295, 1480, 1665, 1850, 2035, 2220) m of sport yarn

US4/3.5 mm circular needles, 32-inch/80 cm and 23-inch/60 cm (or size needed to achieve gauge)

US2/2.75 mm circular needle, 23-inch/60 cm (or approximately 0.75 mm smaller than gauge needle)

Spare smaller circular needles for tubular bind-off

Tapestry needle, stitch markers, stitch holders or waste yarn

GAUGE

23 sts x 34 rnds = 4 inches/10 cm in Stockinette stitch with larger needle, after blocking

30 sts x 34 rnds = 4 inches/10 cm in Twisted Rib with larger needle, after blocking

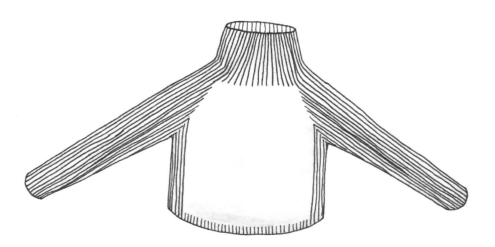

Finished Measurements
Bust: 34½ (38½, 42½, 46½, 50½, 54½, 58½) inches/88 (98, 108, 118, 128, 138, 148) cm
Length (without collar): 16 (16, 16½ , 16½ , 16½, 17, 17) inches/40 (41, 42, 43, 43, 44, 44) cm
Length (with collar): 24 (24½, 24½, 25½ , 25½, 27, 27) inches/60 (61, 62, 65, 65, 68, 68) cm
Collar circumference: 22 (24, 24, 25½ , 25½, 27, 27) inches/56 (60, 60, 64, 64, 68, 68) cm
Sleeve length from underarm: 17 (17, 17, 18, 18, 18½ , 18½) inches/43 (44, 44, 46, 46, 47, 47) cm
Upper arm sleeve circumference: 10½ (11½, 12, 13, 14, 16, 17) inches/27 (29, 31, 34, 36.5, 40.5, 43) cm
Wrist sleeve circumference: 8 (8, 8, 9, 9, 10, 10) inches/20 (20, 20, 22, 22, 24, 24) cm

De Rerum Natura
Toulouse, France
dererumnatura.fr
@dererumnatura

COLLAR

Using smaller needles and the Italian tubular cast-on method (see p. 66), CO 168 (180, 180, 192, 192, 204, 204) sts. Join in the rnd being careful not to twist and pl mBOR.
Set-up Rnd 1: (Sl1 wyif, k1) to end of rnd.
Set-up Rnd 2: (P1, sl1 wyib) to end of rnd.
Set-up Rnd 3: (Sl1 wyif, k1-tbl) to end of rnd.
Set-up Rnd 2: (P1, sl1 wyib) to end of rnd.
Change to larger needles.
Rnd 1: (P1, k1-tbl) to end of rnd.
Repeat this last rnd until work measures 8 (8, 8, 9, 9, 10, 10) inches/20 (20, 20, 22, 22, 24, 24) cm from cast-on edge.

BODY

Rnd 1: *(K1, sl1 wyib) 25 (28, 30, 32, 33, 34, 35) times, k1, pl m, 5-inc, (p1, k1-tbl) 15 (15, 13, 14, 13, 15, 14) times, p1, 5-inc*, pl m. Repeat from * to * once more—184 (196, 196, 208, 208, 220, 220) sts.
Rnd 2: *Knit to m, remove m, k2, pl m, (k1-tbl, p1) to 5 sts before m, k1-tbl, p1, k1-tbl, pl m, k2, remove m.* Repeat from * to * once more.
Rnd 3: *Knit to m, sl m, (k1-tbl, p1) to 1 st before m, k1-tbl, sl m, k2. Repeat from * to * once more.
Rnd 4: Work Rnd 3 once more.
Rnd 5: *Knit to 1 st before m, sl m, 5-inc, p1, (k1-tbl, p1) to 1 st before m, 5-inc, sl m, k2.* Repeat from * to * once more—16 sts inc'd.
Repeat Rounds 2–5 for 8 (10, 12, 14, 16, 18, 20) more times—328 (372, 404, 448, 480, 524, 556) sts.
Repeat Rounds 2–4 once more.

Body/sleeves separation

Next Rnd: *Knit to 2 sts before m, pl m, p1, k1-tbl, remove m, pl next 73 (81, 85, 95, 101, 113, 119) sts onto spare yarn, remove m, CO 7 (7, 7, 7, 7, 9, 9) sts, k1-tbl, p1.* Repeat from * to * once more, pl mBOR—196 (224, 248, 272, 292, 316, 336) sts.
Next Round: *Knit to m, sl m, (p1, k1-tbl) five times, p1.* Repeat from * to * once more.
Repeat this last rnd until body measures 15 (15½, 16, 16½, 16½, 16½, 16½) inches/38 (39, 40, 41, 41, 42, 42) cm down the back from beginning of St st section.
Next Rnd: Using smaller needles, (k1-tbl, p1) to end.
Repeat this last rnd seven more times.
Bind off using smaller needles and the Tubular Bind-Off method (see p. 66).

SLEEVES

Pl 73 (81, 85, 95, 101, 113, 119) sleeve sts back onto larger needle.
Rnd 1 (RS): (K1-tbl, p1) to last st, k1-tbl, pl m, pick up and knit 7 (7, 7, 7, 7, 9, 9) sts from underarm, pl mBOR, join to knit in the rnd—80 (88, 92, 102, 108, 122, 128) sts.
Rnd 2: (K1-tbl, p1) to end.
Repeat Rnd 2 five more times.
**Decrease Rnd:* 3-decL, p1, (k1-tbl, p1) to 3 sts before m, 3-decR, p1, (k1-tbl, p1) to end—4 sts dec'd.
Repeat Rnd 2 until work measures 2¾ (2¼, 2, 1¾, 1½, 1¼, 1¼) inches/7 (6, 5, 4.5, 4, 3.5, 3.5) cm from previous Decrease Rnd.*
Repeat from * to * 3 (5, 6, 7, 8, 10, 11) more times—64 (64, 64, 70, 72, 78, 80) sts.
Repeat Decrease Rnd once more—60 (60, 60, 66, 68, 74, 76) sts.
Repeat Rnd 2 until work measures 17 (17, 17, 18, 18, 18½, 18½) inches/43 (44, 44, 46, 46, 47, 47) cm from underarm.
Bind off using smaller needles and the Tubular Bind-Off technique.
Repeat for second sleeve.

Finishing

Weave in ends and block to finished measurements.

Julie loves Paris

Favorite (movies, songs, books, tv shows)

Top of my list is **Lady Gaga**. I discovered her music when I started designing, and I need my daily dose of Gaga as much as I need knitting every day. I identify with her as a female artist and as a vulnerable yet strong woman, and I love that each of her albums has a different mood, a different style, yet is so unmistakably hers. This is what I want to achieve with my designs: always find new ideas, change techniques, colors and styles, yet stay true to my identity as a designer.

Jane Austen: I'm a *Pride and Prejudice* nerd. Read it countless times; read the sequels, prequels, and spoofs; watched all the movies and series!

The Devil Wears Prada: Girly, feel-good, somehow fashion related, yes please! But basically, give me a Meryl Streep movie anytime!

Black Books: My go-to comedy series, I've watched it so many times I can quote whole episodes by heart.

The Wire: An absolute must! The best series ever! From the plot to the soundtrack!

Métro knitting: must-have or never ever?

Métro knitting is totally fine as long as you avoid rush hour! Pointy needles can be life hazards in an overcrowded Métro car, trust me! At any other time, you can freely get your needles out and knit away. It can even be an ice-breaker, if you're in luck!

Picker or thrower?

I'm a thrower, like most French knitters. Throwing was considered patriotic in the 20th century because picking was the German way of knitting. When I was six, I spent a whole week at my grandparents' because I was not allowed to go back to school until all signs of chickenpox had disappeared from my body. This is the blessed week when my grandmother taught me to tie my shoes and to knit. I made doll blankets and, years later, a very long but miserably narrow ribbed scarf that I nevertheless wore with pride in high school.

Project monogamy or cast on all the things?

Cast on all the things! I need several projects on my needles at all times, so I can knit every day! Mindless oceans of stocking stitch for knit nights or train journeys, desk projects that require my undivided attention, handbag socks…

Favorite places to eat/drink/knit in Paris?

I take my kids to **Manga Café** in the 13°, where I can knit while they read. Couches and cushioned cubicles are knitter-friendly, and you can grab a Japanese bite to eat while you're there.

La butte aux piafs in the 13° has great fancy burgers and serves beer that is brewed in Paris.

Hotel Grand Amour has an outdoor patio within the restaurant where you can spend hours after your lunch without ever feeling unwelcome, just down the street from **Les Tricoteurs Volants**.

Cesar Italian restaurant two minutes away from **Lil Weasel**.

Saigon Moi in the 13° is a Vietnamese restaurant serving yummy green papaya salad, bo bun, and pho.

Vivienne Beret

by Sylvie Polo/Polo & Co.

What is more French than a béret? With archaeology and art history revealing examples of bérets since the Bronze Age, it was in the 17th century in Southern France that production of Basque-style bérets began, and the first béret factory has records dating back to 1810. What started as traditional headgear for shepherds in the Pyrenees became the hat of the working classes in the 1920s. While some may consider it a stereotype, people throughout France still wear berets in the 21st century.

Vivienne is a lovely fair isle colorwork project, a very feminine version of the classic béret. The colorwork highlights the long-standing connection between France and Scotland, while the shape of the béret is that of the Basque region stretching across southern France and northern Spain.

Knit up this lovely example and wear your béret with pride (though perhaps not with your stripe-y shirt—let's not be too cliché).

SIZE

S (M, L) to fit head circumference 19¼ (21, 23) inches/49 (53.25, 58.5) cm with brim stretched, shown in size M

MATERIALS

C1: Polo & Co. Rustique Fine (100% Wool; 437 yd/400 m per 100 g skein); Color: Rose Antique; 1 skein or approximately 80 m of fingering yarn

C2: Polo & Co. Meygal (50% Camel, 50% Merino; 437 yd/400 m per 100 g skein); Color: Natural; 1 skein or approximately 80 m of fingering yarn

C3: Polo & Co. Masgot Fine (100% Wool; 437 yd/400 m per 100 g skein); Color: Silex; 1 skein or approximately 80 m of fingering yarn

C4: Polo & Co. Masgot Fine Craie (100% Wool; 437 yd/400 m per 100 g skein); Color: Craie; 1 skein or approximately 80 m of fingering yarn

US4/3.5 mm circular needle, 16-inch/40 cm + set of DPNs (or size needed to achieve gauge)

US0/2.5 mm circular needle, 16-inch/40 cm (or approximately 1.0 mm smaller than gauge needle)

Stitch marker, tapestry needle

GAUGE

26 sts x 32 rows = 4 inches/10 cm in Stockinette stitch with larger needle, after blocking

Finished Measurements
Diameter: 10 (11, 12) inches/26 (29, 31) cm
Brim Circumference: 17¼ (19, 21) inches/43.75 (48.25, 53.25) cm, unstretched

Polo & Co.
Normandy, France
etsy.com/shop/PoloandCo
@poloetcie

BRIM

With C1 and smaller needle, CO 112 (124, 136) stitches using, join in the rnd being careful not to twist, pl mBOR.

Rnd 1: Knit all sts. Join in C2.

Rnd 2: *K1 in C1, p1 in C2; repeat from * to end of rnd.

Work in pattern for eight rnds. Break C2.

BODY

Change to larger needle.

Rnd 1: Using C1, *k2, m1; repeat from * to end of rnd—168 (186, 204) sts

Rnd 2: Work Chart 1 for 28 (31, 34) times around for 30 rnds of chart.

CROWN

Setup for Size Small: *K28, m1, pl m; repeat from six times total—174 sts.

Setup for Sizes Medium (Large): *K31 (34), pl m; repeat from * six times total.

For all sizes, continue colorwork with Chart 2:

Rnd 1: *K2tog, work from Chart 2 to 2 sts before m, ssk; repeat from * six times to end of rnd—12 sts dec'd.

Rnd 2: Work from Chart 2 to end of rnd.

Repeat Rnds 1&2 for 13 (14, 15) times total, proceeding to Chart 3 for your size after Rnd 18—18 (18, 24) sts. Change to DPNs when sts no longer fit comfortably on needle. Break C3.

Next Rnd: With C1, *k1, k2tog; repeat from * to end of rnd—12 (12, 16) sts.

STEM

Next Rnd: K2tog to end of rnd—6 (6, 8) sts.

For Sizes Small (Medium): K2tog to end of rnd—3 (3) sts.

For Size Large: K2tog, s2kpo twice—3 sts.

For all sizes: Work I-cord (see p. 66) for 1 inch/2.5 cm.

Break yarn leaving a 6-inch tail. Thread end onto tapestry needle and pull through remaining sts to close.

Finishing

Weave in all ends. Wet your tam in warm water with a tiny amount of shampoo added, squeeze gently to remove excess water, then stretch over a plate (the base of the plate to the top wheel of the tam). Rest plate on a vase or upturned bowl and leave to dry completely.

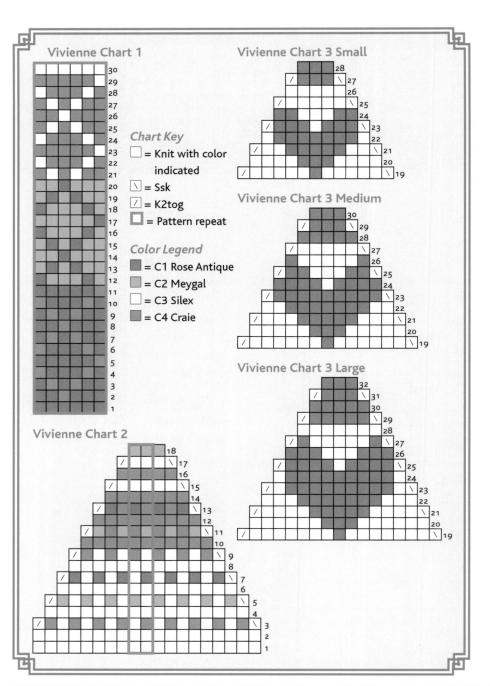

Vivienne Chart 1

Vivienne Chart 3 Small

Vivienne Chart 3 Medium

Vivienne Chart 3 Large

Vivienne Chart 2

Chart Key

☐ = Knit with color indicated

╲ = Ssk

╱ = K2tog

☐ = Pattern repeat

Color Legend

■ = C1 Rose Antique

■ = C2 Meygal

☐ = C3 Silex

■ = C4 Craie

Sylvie loves Paris

What has your knitwear design journey been like?
I just wake up with an idea! Or sometimes the yarn gives me the idea and the design, but I work a lot by instinct and the sensation that the color provides me. I barely make a drawing.

Tell us about a Paris hidden treasure (or three)...
La Ruche (literally, The Beehive), an artists' residence in the 15°, which was opened early in the 20th century and was home to Chagall, Brâncusi, Modigliani, and more. While the studios are not open to the public, the neighborhood and the hive-shaped building itself are worth a visit.
Rue Mouzaïa in the 19° with all the small, charming villas and cobblestone streets.
Les Catacombes de Paris in the 14°! Skulls and bones of six million Parisians disinterred from their overflowing cemeteries were stacked into patterns to create an underground ossuary.

Top Five Movies
1. *La folie des grandeurs* 2. *Les Tontons flingueurs* 3. *Star Wars (all of it!)* 4. *The Lord of the Rings* 5. *The Hobbit*

Métro knitting: must-have or never ever?
Never ever knitted in the Métro—too crowded! I'm a train knitter.

Favorite station?
I don't have a favorite station—I don't like the Métro. Get me back to Normandy!

Favorite neighborhood?
Parc des Buttes Chaumont—I love this garden in the 19°.

Picker or thrower?
Project monogamie or cast on all the things?
Thrower. Monogamie.

Favorite place to eat in Paris?
New Balal Indian restaurant near Les Galeries Lafayette in the 9°.

Christelle Bagéa

Email: christelle@tricotetstitch.com
Instagram: @tricot_et_stitch
Ravelry: Tricot & Stitch

Under the **Tricot & Stitch** umbrella, Christelle loves to design knitting patterns, mainly shawls and socks, dye a bit of yarn, host her podcast, and organize fun knitting events. She aims to spread the love and make knitting a fulfilling and fun experience for all knitters. She lives with her husband and four kids near Paris, in a cozy home where she hoards lots of yarn, fiber, books, tea, and all sorts of cross stitch notions. You can find her at *tricotetstitch.com*.

Enrico Castronovo

Email: contact@lestricoteursvolants.com
Instagram: @lestricoteursvolants
Ravelry: Les Tricoteurs Volants

One evening in the year 2007, Enrico learnt to knit from a knitting friend. Since then, his life has never been the same. He started accumulating yarn, as well as needles (with his black cat's delight), and one thing became important in his eyes: knitting. Oh, and crochet, spinning, weaving, dying, and sewing. A few years later, he left his work as a bookseller and his financial safety to open his own yarn store in Paris, **Les Tricoteurs Volants** (The Flying Knitters). Since then, he spends his days rolling himself in yarn and listening to weird music, but also serving and assisting his customers, who appreciate his proficiency, skills, and good advice. From time to time, Enrico has gotten a more-or-less original idea for a sweater, a shawl, or another knitted item, and then he dares to share it on Ravelry. Find him at *lestricoteursvolants.com*.

Marion Crivelli

Email: marion63550@gmail.com
Instagram: @marionknits
Ravelry: Marion-Knits

Marion lives in the center of France. She loves Paris for its architecture, its museums. After test knitting for years for several designers, she decided to create her own pattern. She loves testing new materials, colors made by the dyers. That's what inspires her. Seeing her designs worked up by other knitters is her best reward.

Julie Dubreux

Email: julieknitsinparis@gmail.com
Instagram: @julieknitsinparis
Ravelry: julieknitsinparis

Julie Dubreux is a French knitwear designer and knitting instructor. Her enthusiastic love for the knitting community translates into colorful collaborations with indie dyers from all around the world. Her designs have been published in *Pom Pom Quarterly*.

Chloé Fourtune-Ravard

Email: patterns@tisserincoquet.fr
Instagram: @tisserin_coquet
Ravelry: ParticuleAlpha

Chloé comes from a family of crafters and learned to embroider at a very early age. It developed her love for thread, fabric, and yarn which has not left her since. She was born and lived in Paris for almost all her life, spending hours on Paris public transportation every day, allowing her to knit extensively. She soon started designing her own patterns to play and experiment with colors and textures. She focuses on original but simple patterns with a wow factor, as she believes every knitter can tackle any technique, if it's properly explained. She is also a knitting teacher, helping knitters to conquer advanced techniques without headaches. She can be found at *tisserincoquet.fr* or hiding unexpected new additions to her stash in her secret closet.

Lucile Francomme

Email: contact@lucileateliersdesigns.com
Instagram: @lucileateliersdesigns
Ravelry: LucileAD

Lucile has played with yarn since early childhood, and needles are common tools in her family. For more than three years, she practiced knitting very intensely with great enthusiasm. She decided to make this passion her main activity by becoming a knitting teacher and an independent designer. Yarn is an amazing material that can be valued in an infinite number of ways. Lucile is always on the lookout for new techniques to discover in order to master them more and more and, above all, to teach them in the best way during her classes and in her patterns. You can find her at *lucileateliersdesigns.com*.

Marie-Amélie

Email: maremelade@gmail.com
Instagram: @maremelade
Ravelry: Marie Amélie Designs

Passionate about fashion and enthusiastic about creating things from her hands, Marie-Amélie fell in love with knitting at the moment she discovered all the beautiful garments she could make simply with a thread, two knitting needles, and an inspiring pattern. Through the patterns she creates, Marie-Amélie shares with customers her taste for modern and feminine garments. She loves to introduce new techniques to them with interesting details and polished finishing and make them not only feel proud to have knitted one of her patterns but also to wear what they have made.

Sara Maternini

Email: info@lacavealaine.com
Instagram: @lacavealaine
Ravelry: La Cave à Laine

Sara Maternini is the founder and designer of **La Cave à Laine**, modern knitting patterns and accessories for knitters. Sara is Italian and lives with her family in Alsace, France. She began to knit when she was seven, but only later in life did she transform it into a passion and then a job. She is partial to all shades of grey and blue, the right amount of pinks, and all the other colors of the world. She loves to help knitters accomplish their dream shawls in style while having fun. She collects stitch dictionaries, books by Elizabeth Zimmermann, and hand dyed yarns. You can find her at *lacavealaine.com*.

Sylvie Polo

Email: poloetcie@orange.fr
Instagram: @poloetcie
Ravelry: Polo Sylvie

Sylvie Polo is an independent designer who works for famous perfumers. She is fortunate to work at home with her husband in their office, which gives her time for her two girls and, of course, for knitting. They chose to live in the countryside in a small village in Normandy with few inhabitants but many cows, lots of milk and cheese! She has knitted since childhood, when her grandmother taught her. She also hand dyes yarn as **Polo & Co.** on Etsy. You can find her yarn at *etsy.com/shop/PoloandCo.*

Kathleen Dames

Email: kathleen@onemorerowpress.com
Instagram: @kathleendames
Ravelry: Purly

Though she does not speak French *per se*, Kathleen is fluent in knitting, fashion, ballet, and food, so she gets by in the City of Light. With a focus on flattering designs and knitterly details, she designs garments and accessories for her own pattern line, as well as publications such as *Knitty*, *Jane Austen Knits*, and *Interweave Knits*. From her first large-scale knitting project,

Kathleen has been making patterns her own, thanks to her personal style, the wisdom of Elizabeth Zimmermann, and the stacks of stitch dictionaries she keeps buying. On top of designing, Kathleen is cocreator of the knitting publication *Filament*, host of the podcast *The Sweater with Kathleen Dames*, and cofounder with Alice O'Reilly of One More Row Press. Find more at *kathleendames.com.*

Clara Ferrand

Instagram: @clarafotomania

Clara is a photographer of fashion but also of intensity, it is the look, the movement of the body, the agreement of space and time. She does not look for timelessness, but on the contrary, the power of the present, the second of this unique moment that she can

see and imprison forever and for everyone. She is a painter who, in a flash and without a brush, covers the world of magic, where we do not conceive ordinary banality, a thousand times seen, but never watched. Find more at *ferrandclara.com.*

Alice O'Reilly

Email: alice@onemorerowpress.com
Instagram: @backyardfiberworks
Ravelry: AliceOKnitty

Alice has always been a maker. A serious dyed in the wool, hot glue burns on her fingertips, glitter in her eyebrows maker. So when she first thought about dyeing yarn, it was in the context of making stuff to support her knitting habit. She fired up her first dye pot and, wow, was it not what she expected. True to form, she did no research. It was way too light and way too dark and way too not what was expected. But, also true to form, she kept trying. Alice threw a few more skeins in the pot. She read a few (okay a lot, she works at a library) of books about dyeing and yarn and how the two work together. Alice joined Ravelry groups and marveled at everyone else's perfect skeins. She started stalking hand-dyers on Instagram and Etsy. And then slowly she started getting more predictable results. More repeatable colorways. And it turns out she loved playing with color as much as she loved playing with yarn. And that's how **Backyard Fiberworks** began. Check out more of her yarn at *backyardfiberworks.com*

Thanks!

Laura Cameron—technical editor

Alisson Corteggiani—model

Lucile Francomme—stylist

Laurel Johnson—illustrator

Our family & friends
for their love and support

The City of Paris & Tricoteurs Everywhere

BOR = beginning of round
CC = contrasting color
CN = cable needle
CO = cast on
cont = continue; continuing
dec('d) = decrease(d)
DPN(s) = double pointed needle(s)
foll = follow(s); following
inc('d) = increase(d)
k = knit
kfb = knit into front and back of the same stitch—1 st inc'd
k-wise = knit-wise
k2tog = knit two stitches together—1 st dec'd
m = marker
m1/2/3/4 = marker 1/2/3/4
mC = cable marker
MC = main color
m1-F = Lifted Increase = insert left needle under strand between 2 stitches from the back, then lift strand onto left needle and knit through back loop—1 st inc'd
m1-L = make one stitch using backwards loop over the right needle—1 st inc'd

m1-Lp = make one purled stitch using backwards loop—1 st inc'd
m1-R = make one stitch using backwards loop twisted in the opposite direction of m1-L—1 st inc'd
m1-Rp = make one purled stitch using backwards loop twisted in the opposite direction of m1-Lp—1 st inc'd
M2 = Double lifted increase = insert left needle tip from front to back under the bar between stitches, lifting it to form a new loop on left needle, (k1-tbl, p1) in this loop—2 sts inc'd
p = purl
patt(s) = pattern(s)
pfb = purl into front and back of the same stitch—1 st inc'd
pl = place
p-wise = purl-wise
p2tog = purl two together—1 st dec'd
rep = repeat
RS = right side
sl = slip stitch purl-wise to right needle
ssk = slip two stitches individually, then knit them together—1 st dec'd

ssp = slip two stitches individually purl-wise, then purl them together through the back loops—1 st dec'd
st(s) = stitch(es)
s2kpo = slip two stitches together knit-wise, knit one stitch, pass two slipped stitches over—2 sts dec'd
-tbl = through the back loop(s)
WS = wrong side
wyib = with yarn in back
wyif = with yarn in front
W&T = Wrap and Turn = bring yarn to front of work between needles, slip next stitch purl-wise to right needle, bring yarn around this stitch to back of work, slip stitch back to left needle, turn work
yo = yarnover—1 st inc'd
5-inc = (k1, yo, k1, yo, k1) into the same stitch—4 sts inc'd
3-decL = slip one stitch, knit two stitches together, pass slipped stitch over—2 sts dec'd
3-decR = slip one stitch, knit one stitch, pass slipped stitch over, pass next stitch over—2 sts dec'd

Stitches

Garter Stitch (worked flat)
Knit all sts, all rows.

Garter Stitch (in the round)
Rnd 1: Knit all sts.
Rnd 2: Purl all sts.

Reverse Stockinette Stitch (worked flat)
Row 1 (RS): Purl all sts.
Row 2 (WS): Knit all sts.

Reverse Stockinette Stitch (in the round)
Purl all sts, all rnds.

Stockinette Stitch (worked flat)
Row 1 (RS): Knit all sts.
Row 2 (WS): Purl all sts.

Stockinette Stitch (in the round)
Knit all sts, all rnds.

2/1 Twisted Rib (worked flat)
Row 1 (RS): *K2-tbl, p1; rep from * to end.
Row 2 (WS): *K1, p2-tbl; rep from * to end.

Techniques

Cabling without a cable needle
youtube.com/watch?v=-6DB6WhAKvY

Emily Ocker's Circular Beginning
youtube.com/watch?v=MIFq29Dq6zU

Italian Tubular Cast-On
newstitchaday.com/the-italian-cast-on-knitting/

I-cord (worked over 3 sts)
Step 1: K3 sts on DPN.
Step 2: Sl3 sts to other end of DPN.
Repeat Steps 1&2 as specified in pattern.

I-cord Bind-Off
Step 1: K2 sts, k2tog-tbl (last st of i-cord with next st of main piece).
Step 2: Sl3 sts back to left needle.
Repeat Steps 1&2 as specified in pattern.

Jeny's Suprisingly Stretchy Bind-Off
knitty.com/ISSUEfall09/FEATjssbo.php

Kitchener stitch
newstitchaday.com/kitchener-stitch/
Bring tapestry needle through front st as if to purl, back st as if to knit, *front st as if to knit then remove stitch from knitting needle, next front st as if to purl, back st as if to purl then remove st from knitting needle, next back st as if to knit; repeat from * to end.

Magic Loop
youtube.com/watch?v=_dDHKcY2x0g

Tubular Bind-Off
Set-up Rnd 1: (K1-tbl, sl1 wyif) to end.
Set-up Rnd 2: (Sl1 wyib, p1) to end.
Repeat these 2 rnds once more.
Hold 2 spare circular needles in your right hand, transfer all the knit sts to the needle at the front, and all the purl sts to the needle at the back.
Graft sts together using Kitchener stitch.

Pattern Index

Bon Tricot!

CPSIA information can be obtained
at www.ICGtesting.com
Printed in the USA
BVHW06n1055270918
528486BV00003B/27/P